Wallasey

Now and Then

The Family History Society of Cheshire

Wallasey Group

20th Anniversary 1990-2010

Researchers and Co-authors:

Wendy Bennett, Irene Birch, Paul Davies and Sheila Hamilton

The History of Wallasey Group of the FHS of Cheshire   Helen M Gill

Photographers:

Wendy Bennett, Irene Birch, Paul Davies and Sheila Hamilton

Photographic Editor:

Wendy Bennett

Editor:

Irene Birch

First Published 2010 by Countyvise Limited,
14 Appin Road, Birkenhead, Wirral CH41 9HH.

Copyright © 2010 The Wallasey Group of the Family History Society of Cheshire

The right of The Wallasey Group of the Family History Society of Cheshire to be identified as editors of this work has been asserted by them in accordance with the Copyright, Design and Patents Act 1988.

British Library Cataloguing in Publication Data.
A catalogue record for this book is available from the British Library.

ISBN 978 1 906823 34 4

Thanks

My special thanks go to my co-authors who have given their full support to this venture. Their interest and enthusiasm has been remarkable, enabling us to work as a team to produce this book. Wendy's expertise with the photographic editing has been invaluable and Sheila and Paul have done wonders with the information that we have all gleaned. I would also like to thank Helen for her comprehensive history of the Group. This is our first attempt at such a project.

To Jenny Done and Diane Whittaker at Wallasey Reference Library I would like to say a special thank you. They have been so helpful and supportive throughout our months of research and have assisted us in every possible way, in our search for facts. My thanks go also to everyone else who has contributed in any way to our book.

I would also like to thank our long-suffering spouses and families for their help and encouragement during this mammoth task. They have had to put up with the endless piles of papers, photographs, and general disruption that we have caused. Maybe life will return to normal now that it is complete.

We hope that you will enjoy reading our book and perhaps discover something new about Wallasey in the process. We began our project unsure of whether we would find enough material to fill sufficient pages. In the event we need not have worried, there was more than we could use.

Most of the new photographs have been taken by us during 2009 and 2010.

Irene Birch
Group Leader
Editor

Acknowledgements for Photographs

We wish to thank everyone for their generosity by contributing their photographs for inclusion in our book. The photographs have come from collections large and small and also individual photographs with special memories. They have each helped to bring the story of the Wallasey area to life. During the process of collecting our information we have acquired some photographs whose origins we have not been able to confirm and therefore we would like to apologise in advance if we have not acknowledged them.

Wallasey Reference Library Photographic Collection

Wirral Archives

Courtesy of National Museums of Liverpool (Stewart Bale Collection) Merseyside

Maritime Museum

Courtesy of Cinema Theatre Association Archive

Courtesy of Cinema Theatre Association Archive Tony Moss Collection

Courtesy of Nautilus International (Mariners' Park)

Wendy Bennett Collection

Ken Clark Collection

Mike Colebourne Collection

Sheila Fidler Collection

Foulger Collection

Clive Garner Collection

C Greenwood Collection

Sheila Hamilton Collection

Harry Nickson Collection

Priestley Collection

Jim Rogers Collection

Thomas G Turner Collection

Geoff Baker

David Britton

Irene Cunningham

Margaret Dann

Paul Davies

Walter Forsyth

Roger and Helen Gill

Angela Goodman

Robin Nettleton

Michael Parker

Brian Perry

Sheila and David Pugh

Barbara Reid

Jim Varty

Alan Wilkinson

Bibliography

Wallasey Reference Library Local Folders Collection including newspaper cuttings etc...

The Rise and Progress of Wallasey   E C Woods and P C Brown

Notes in the History of Wallasey   E C Woods, P C Brown and H Hopps

The History of the Hundred of Wirral 1847   W W Mortimer

Landmarks of Old Wallasey Village 1859   Thomas Westcott

Growth of Wallasey and Future Development (A Thesis) 1936   W B Thorp

Picture House Magazine No.7 1985   Cinemas of Wallasey   Clive Garner

The Story of Mariner' Park 1999 NUMAST   (Ian & Marilyn Boumphrey)

Jonathan Bennison 1835 Liverpool Map (Wallasey area)

1837 to 1851 Tithe Maps and Apportionments

Ordnance Survey Maps 1875, 1898 and 1909

Gore's and Kelly's Directories

Census Returns

Contents

Introduction

The idea for the publication of this book was born as the result of the forthcoming 20th anniversary of the Wallasey Group of the Family History Society of Cheshire.

The inaugural meeting was held in March 1990 and, due to the continued interest in researching family history, has gone from strength to strength. This is in no small part due to the support of our many members throughout this time. It is a testament to their enthusiasm and interest, that we are able to achieve such a lasting memento of the Group's achievements over the years.

Wallasey, as we know it, is made up of the three original villages that covered the northern part of the Hundred of Wirral, namely, Poulton cum Seacombe, Liscard and Wallasey, all of which are located to the north of the banks of the old Wallasey Pool and the River Birket which forms a natural boundary, separating Wallasey from Birkenhead.

Between 1801 and 1841 the combined population of Poulton cum Seacombe increased from 178 to 2446. At the same time the population of Liscard rose from 967 to 2873 and that of Wallasey from 274 to 942.

As the 19th century progressed, so did the expansion of these villages. As a result, we will cover Poulton and Seacombe in separate chapters.

Egremont which linked Seacombe and Liscard developed from 1829, when Captain John Askew purchased the ferry and named it, together with the surrounding area, Egremont, after his birthplace in Cumberland.

In 1830 Mr James Atherton, a retired merchant of Liverpool, purchased 170 acres of sand hills and rocky outcrops at the northernmost tip of the Wirral with the intention of creating a high class residential area close to the sea with its healthy climate, naming it after Brighton in Sussex, thus New Brighton and Upper Brighton were born.

Each of these villages gradually spread outwards as the population grew and now it is sometimes quite difficult to identify the boundaries between them, thus the whole area is known as Wallasey and New Brighton.

It was not until 1928 that Leasowe and Moreton were incorporated, followed in 1933 by Saughall Massie. These last three were formerly part of the parish of Bidston cum Ford.

The book cannot be a definitive record of all the changes that have occurred but we have tried to create a balanced record for future reference.

Whilst compiling the contents it has become apparent that a natural course of evolution is taking place.

The original villages were more or less self-contained. As the population grew, during the 19th century, house building expanded to accommodate the influx of artisans who were needed for the growing industries. As a result there were more and more demands upon the facilities. More goods and services were required and houses in many main streets were converted into shops to cater for the new inhabitants. Corner shops sprang up everywhere. Shopping locally was the norm. Close-knit communities developed and they had everything they needed "on the doorstep".

A rapid reversal has now begun. Because most families have their own cars, shopping is moving away from the High Street, to purpose built town centre and out-of-town Supermarkets and Retail Parks. As a result more and more small shops are closing, the shop fronts are disappearing and the shops are reverting to use as houses. Unfortunately, the conversions have not always been carried out sympathetically. Everything changes with time.

There were many churches, of different denominations, throughout the area. Sadly, due to falling congregations, many have closed and the buildings have either been demolished or converted to other uses.

A similar situation happened to the many cinemas. At the height of their popularity some 60 years ago, there were 13 cinemas scattered throughout the borough, now there are none. With the advent of television and video recording people can enjoy similar entertainment in their own homes. Many cinemas changed to Bingo Halls, were adapted for other activities or just closed down. The only cinemas we have now are multi-screen, purpose-built complexes located, mainly, in the new Retail Parks.

It is pleasing to see that new 21st century buildings are once again showing signs of the architects' and bricklayers' skills. More decorative designs are replacing the drab concrete boxes that were so prolific in the post-war years. Sadly, in Wallasey, even these post-war developments have not stood the test of time and are gradually being replaced.

This is why it is so important to preserve a record of what has survived until the early 21st century. What will be the legacy in another 100 years?

CHAPTER ONE

The History of The Wallasey Group of the FHS of Cheshire

Wallasey Group started out as a local Family History Society founded by K. S. Sheel at a time when the Family History Society of Cheshire had only two Wirral Groups: one at Birkenhead which met in the afternoon and the other at Bebington which met in the evening. The inaugural meeting was held on the 5th April 1989 at 8 pm in the Community Room at the CVS, Liscard Road, where a surprising number of twenty-six people arrived for the meeting.

Less than twelve months later, Mr. Sheel felt unable to continue in office and a plea for support was sent out to the FHS of Cheshire. Fortunately they were only too keen to embrace the idea and The Wallasey Group of the Family History Society of Cheshire was born. Its first appearance in *The Journal of the Family History Society of Cheshire*, as the Cheshire Ancestor was formerly known, was in June 1990 and reads: *The Society's newly-formed Wallasey Group was welcomed by the Society's Chairman, Mr. David Lambert, who then gave an interesting talk on the works of the Society. Group officers were then elected.*

Those first officers were voted in as follows: Group Leader, Monica Hart; Secretary/Treasurer, Louise Phillips; Microfilm, Mike King; Census, Nancy Treleaven; Library, Margaret Jackson.

Monica was, I believe, the driving force behind the successful rescue bid and when she stood down, three years later, she remained an active group member, and continued, for some time, to provide the much appreciated tea and biscuits at our meetings. Sadly, Monica died in 2004 but will be fondly remembered not only for the help she gave to others but also for her steadfast dedication to the group as a whole.

Anne Evans took over from Monica for a short while then became our Treasurer for a number of years until her marriage in 2004, after which she moved down south to set up home with her new husband. Our third Group Leader, Annie Weare, served only a brief term with us. She had come over from Australia intending to remain in this country for some time, however, her planned stay was cut short and she reluctantly left us to return to the Antipodes.

Mike King then took over the reins, and it is also Mike we have to thank for looking after the Group's interests in organising the rota for the Society's circulating microfiche, right from the beginning. This service is now much underused, most newcomers preferring to search on the Internet, but Mike stalwartly continues to coordinate with the other groups of the Society to provide this facility, which we in Wallasey fought for, so valiantly, back in the days before any of us had a home computer!

Next came Wendy Bennett, our longest serving Group Leader, with a creditable eight years of service in total. Wendy has not only led us enthusiastically in the past but has also stepped into the breach, in times of crisis, on more than one occasion as acting Group Leader. It was also Wendy who introduced us to the Wallasey Group Newsletter, a lively mix of local and national family history news in glorious technicolour.

Meanwhile our venue in Liscard was proving a trial in a number of ways: double yellow lines outside meant parking some distance away and carrying equipment was proving a headache; also there was the question of someone having to pick up the key to the rooms beforehand on the day of the meeting. Other venues were considered, and Barbara Reid and Anne Evans suggested Egremont Presbyterian Church in Manor Road, now known as the Manor Church Centre. Both members of the church, they arranged a hiring of the room at a very attractive rate, which included storage facilities for our growing library, although parking was somewhat limited on the main road outside. This was fine for a short while,

(L to R) Ann Evans, Mike Colebourne, Helen Gill, Mike King, Barbara Reid, Monica Hart, Irene Birch and Liz Murray at Wallasey Group's 10th Anniversary Party.

however, it soon became apparent that frequently there would be a conflict of bookings and we would find ourselves, at the last minute, moved to a much smaller room. Not ideal!

In the meantime, changes were taking place in the old mansion house next door to the church. Built in 1848 by Henry Pooley, it was purchased by the YMCA in 1899. More importantly they had a choice of rooms for hire although it would cost us a lot more than we were paying at the church. We moved to the YMCA at around the time Dave Beck became Group Leader, and have been there ever since. The room is generously proportioned and is light and airy with a small kitchen at one end and there is also the convenience of parking within the grounds. Jo McCourt organised a grant from the Neighbourhood Regeneration Fund in 2007, and not only were we able to purchase a laptop and projector for the Group's use but we are now in the fortunate position of having half of our room hire paid for by the fund.

Dave Beck was our sixth Group Leader and was also our Secretary for a number of years. Now, in his capacity as Programme Secretary, Dave continues to book us a variety of interesting speakers who have amused, entertained and even enlightened our small but friendly group of members on occasion!

Wendy was back in the driving seat, temporarily of course, for a further four years until Irene Birch, our current leader, volunteered and was voted in in 2008. Irene's term of office came just in time to make plans to celebrate the Group's 20th Anniversary, and following up an original idea by Paul Davies, formed a sub-committee and set to work to produce this book.

Wallasey Group has been blessed with a number of dedicated committee members over the years who have supported the Group Leaders during their periods of office, including our erstwhile librarians, Ian Threlkeld and Keith Foulkes. Latterly, Dave Beck, Wendy Bennett, Mike

Colebourne, Paul Davies, Rona Ellison, Helen and Roger Gill, Sheila Hamilton, Mike King and Barbara Reid continue to support Irene with the same commitment. We must not forget our tea persons, either, and in 2004 Linda and Jack Hoey took over from Roger and Helen Gill. Sadly, Jack died in November 2008 and we now have Colin and Sheila Beynon making the tea.

Projects

Monumental Inscriptions

(L to R) Dave Dyer, Joan Edwards, Barbara Reid, Wendy Bennett,
John Hankey, Helen Gill, Roger Gill, Nancy Treleaven,
Mike Colebourne and Nancy Foster at St. Hilary's, Wallasey.

Wallasey Group has been particularly active as far as projects are concerned and has been involved in recording the monumental inscriptions in no less than ten churchyards in Wirral. Our first challenge, naturally enough, was St. Hilary's churchyard in Wallasey. It was not the first attempt to be made at recording the inscriptions at the ancient parish church, but this time we had a really good enthusiastic team comprising: Wendy Bennett, Bill Buckley, Mike Colebourne, Dave Dyer, Joan Edwards, Roger Gill, John Hankey, Brian Higgins, Barbara Reid and myself, who turned out every Thursday afternoon to do battle, not only with the elements, but also with the dense undergrowth that hindered our progress along the way. Before we started, I was also told that no plan of the graveyard existed, so I drew one up after Roger and Bill measured and plotted the site – there were some 2478 graves in all - although not every one was marked with a stone. Incidentally, I would like to add here that this is the one and only location I have seen a ghost!

It took us twelve months to complete St. Hilary's MIs and the results, which were printed and microfilmed in 1998, have proved invaluable to many. Spurred on by our success, and having had so much fun from our Thursday afternoon jaunts, we moved on to the Catholic Church of St. Alban in the centre of Liscard with a few less volunteers. I was never sure whether the remains of a dead fox found in the undergrowth at St. Hilary's had put some off! Anyway, this was a relatively easy job because not only was the graveyard much smaller, it was beautifully maintained. The parishioners

St. Alban's Churchyard, Liscard

of St. Alban's had taken it upon themselves to restore the once overgrown and neglected plot into a garden of peace and tranquillity after many of the stones had become broken and fallen down. This project, and an earlier road-widening scheme, resulted in a number of stones being re-sited around the perimeter of the garden, all of which were recorded.

St. John's Church, Egremont

We finished St. Alban's in less than twelve months and went on to record the MIs at St. John's, Egremont with the same small team, accompanied by Margaret Worsley one of the members of the church. With only fifty-five stones in evidence we finished the churchyard in record time. St. John's, built in Grecian style and now awaiting an uncertain future, differs from most churches in that the altar faces west. This may have something to do with the fact that Sir John Tobin, who donated the land, wanted the church facing directly down Church Street, in one straight line, to Tobin Street and Egremont Ferry.

Our next project was Christ Church, Moreton, although our numbers were down to six: Wendy, Bill, Joan, Roger, Barbara and myself. This time we were fortunate enough to be given a detailed plan of the graveyard, which included the grave owner's name and number - we couldn't believe our luck! Liz Murray also joined us on occasion here; she and Jean Wylie had been part of an earlier attempt to record the stones. Christ Church is a large extended graveyard with two ashes plots and two further Gardens of Remembrance but it took us under two years to complete, finishing in 2000.

As we had now exhausted all the Wallasey churchyards, we extended our range and continued our weekly MI recording out at Woodchurch. It might be worth mentioning here that our trusty, aged campervan came in very useful for coffee breaks – particularly if the weather was a little inclement – it has been known for us to squeeze in seven at a push! At Woodchurch, the Rector provided us with a plan, and it was here that three members from the newly formed West Kirby Group, Keith and Joan Sharp and Jo Caird, joined our band of six. By December 2001 we had completed churchyard number five.

(L to R) Wendy Bennett, Keith & Joan Sharp, Jo Caird, Barbara Reid, Helen Gill, Bill Buckley, Joan Edwards and Roger Gill at Holy Cross, Woodchurch.

(L to R) Helen Gill, Jo Caird, Joan Edwards, Keith Sharp, Val Rogan, Joan Sharp, Bill Buckley and Roger Gill at Holy Trinity, Hoylake.

Churchyard number six was at Holy Trinity, Hoylake although the church itself had long since gone after having been found structurally unsound in 1976. Wallasey Group took more of a back seat on this project with only Roger, Joan and myself assisting, leaving West Kirby Group, now joined by Val Rogan, to coordinate the recording of the MIs and to input the results. Roger, as always, prepared the finished results and printed them out. Hoylake graveyard, which took just over two years to complete, has a number of interesting memorials: the 'Titanic' is mentioned on one and there are two references to the 'Lusitania'.

Also commemorated here are two known holders of the VC: Lieutenant J. O'Neil and Corporal Frank Lester who was buried in France.

In 2003, towards the end of the Hoylake project, the Friends of Flaybrick Cemetery asked us to advise them on recording the MIs there, and so our happy band of volunteers spent a very pleasant summer recording the first section with them. The Friends then continued the task independently. In the meantime I was told about a number of gravestones in the grounds of The Friends Meeting House in Slatey Road, Birkenhead. A plaque inside the porch reports they were brought from the Burial Ground at The Friends Meeting House, Withens Lane, Wallasey, in 1984 when the premises and land were sold. I duly recorded them but have been

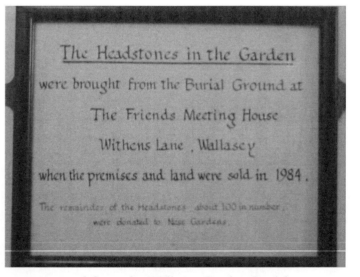

unsuccessful in locating the remainder of the stones removed from the Wallasey Quaker Burial Ground, that were reported to be at Ness Gardens.

When the team, now joined by Heather Chapman, Barbara Dodd and Bill Kelly, arrived at St. John the Divine in Frankby we found it a joy to record, but not much of a challenge - the whole job was done and dusted in five months! This was just as well because our next task was monumental indeed. St. Peter's Churchyard in Heswall had been recorded some years earlier and we were approached to do the checking. This seemed a simple enough task, except for the fact that we were provided only with a print-out. It was far too big a job to OCR (Optical Character Recognition) the whole document and computerise the results in order to produce a book and fiche so we just started again, and recorded the whole graveyard ourselves in our tried and tested way. We had a good set of plans to work with and we finished the job in April 2005 with additional help from John Chapman, Ken Sharpe and Tom Leonard.

We were now travelling a fair distance on our Thursday afternoon expeditions by the time we reached St. Bartholomew's in Thurstaston, and although Rosemary Kirkus joined us here, only Roger and I were left from the original line-up, so we made the decision that once recorded we would call it a day. Rather fittingly, like St. Hilary's in Wallasey, our very first project, St. Bartholomew's too was an ancient site with an old tower in the graveyard from an earlier church. Thurstaston MIs were printed in January 2006 and although we have been asked, since then, to consider recording other churchyards, we have declined.

(Back, L to R) John & Heather Chapman, Tom Leonard, Keith Sharp, Jo Caird, Ken Sharpe, Roger Gill (front) Rosemary Kirkus, Joan Sharp, Helen Gill and Barbara Dodd at St. Bartholomew's, Thurstaston.

One question we had been asked over the years was whether we had recorded the MIs in Wallasey Cemetery in Rake Lane – known by the local comedians as the dead centre of Wallasey! The reply was always the same: because the cemetery was such a big project and the cemetery burial registers are on microfilm, we were concentrating all our efforts on the smaller churchyards – which we were – and there are ten volumes to prove it! Fairly recently, however, Rob Anderson, one of our members, and his wife Rose have recorded the whole of Wallasey Cemetery all by themselves and have deposited a copy of their excellent transcriptions, in nine volumes, in Wallasey Central Library: five Consecrated; three General; one Catholic.

Parish Registers

When, on a personal mission, I eventually discovered the location of the parish registers for Liscard Independent Chapel, later to become Liscard Congregational Church then Liscard URC, the custodian of the registers gave me the opportunity of transcribing them all – baptisms; marriages; burials - and the grave book; this was something of a bonus for me with family connections with the church in the past. In 1995, Roger printed a copy of the transcriptions for use by our Wallasey Group and at the same time, fiche were produced for sale by the Society.

Liscard Independent Chapel

Whilst we were recording the MIs at St. Hilary's, in 1997, the Archivist at the time, Mr. Boase, was looking for someone to type up some handwritten transcripts of the burial registers and

Joan Edwards offered to do the job. We were allowed to keep a printed copy ourselves, for sole use by our Wallasey Group, on condition they were not copied or deposited elsewhere.

Another batch of handwritten transcripts came to light when the son of the late Mr. Ben Pollard was sorting his father's papers, and realising the value of the documents donated them to the Society. They turned out to be transcripts of the parish registers of St. Mary-on-the-Hill, Chester and the Society were looking for someone to input them on to computer. Roger and I were asked to do the baptisms (1547-1831) and burials (1547-1854) which we completed in 1999. Again, there is a printed copy for the Group's use and fiche are available from the Society.

CheshireBMD

At the end of 1999, I was approached by the Society to act as coordinator of the Wirral end of the CheshireBMD project which is a joint project between the county's registration services and family history societies to revolutionise public access to records dating back from the start of Queen Victoria's reign. In 2000, Cheshire's Registration Services became the first county to post their Birth, Marriage and Death records on the Internet.

I hesitated accepting the task only long enough to get Roger's support on the technical side. This was an opportunity not to be missed with me having so many ancestors in the Wallasey district alone! I had been Membership Secretary and Magazine Distributor for the Society from 1989 to 1996, and it was Roger who first computerised the Society's membership list enabling him to print out self-adhesive labels for the envelopes, so I knew that the computer side would not be a problem – for him at any rate!

Our initial visit to the Register Office at Birkenhead Town Hall was a bit of an eye opener after being introduced to the contents of the strong room which was lined from floor to ceiling with metal shelves of tightly packed registers: red for births; green for marriages and black for deaths. The original indexes, some in disrepair after over a century and a half of constant use, were similarly ranged on shelves in the general office. Nothing daunted, I accepted, despite Roger's rough estimate of thirty years work before we even reached 1900!

The indexing process was a steep learning curve on both the Registrar's part and that of us three original volunteers: Roger, Joan Edwards and me. To begin with, we had to squeeze in anywhere the Registrar could find room for us when we arrived for our regular Wednesday morning sessions there – even under the stairs in the basement on one occasion! Also, there were no computers available and so Roger would photocopy the original handwritten indexes, which were then input at home by Joan's husband, George. Once printed out the three of us would check them against the registers. Sounds simple enough, but in the indexes only the first forename appears in full - subsequent names were just an initial. Dates also caused some problems as the indexes used the date of registration not of birth. Consequently, the early days saw us laboriously handwriting in the additional forenames on our printed sheets, and changing dates where necessary, then taking them home to amend on the computer before processing the files for the Internet. This proved so time consuming that we got permission to take in our laptop so at least one of us could input direct from the registers. This certainly speeded things up a bit particularly when we were now permitted to use one of the office computers if it was going spare.

The project really took off once the Archives opened on the first floor of the Town Hall; with three desktop computers available we were able to recruit more volunteers. However, this was dependent on the cooperation of the staff, both upstairs and downstairs, since the opening hours of the Archives were rather restricted which unfortunately resulted in us losing more volunteers than we gained during those early days. Despite this, we reached our primary target of indexing all births, marriages and deaths from 1837 to 1900 by June 2005, and we celebrated with a small party to celebrate the occasion, held in

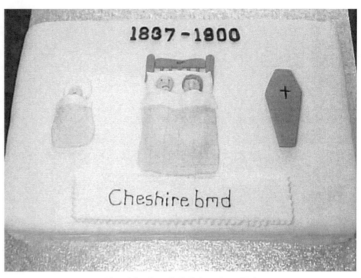

Cheshire bmd Celebration Cake

one of the function rooms at the Town Hall. Many of the church marriages had been indexed previously and were on the Registrar's database, but Roger was kindly allowed a copy these files which he converted into a usable form for the Internet. Amongst our regular volunteers at the Archives were John and Diane Robinson, Margaret Bennett, Irene Birch, Dave Dyer, Veronica Greenwood, Shirley Wynn Jones, Sandra Jones, Joy Keegan, Janette Lyon, Hilda Massey, Sandra Neillie, June Pennell, Peter Williams and Bob Wright.

Once it was on the cards that the Archives were relocating to Cheshire Lines the Registrars had a serious reorganisation and a small office was made available to us with one desktop computer. Now, in addition to two of our own laptops, and a degree of tolerance, up to four volunteers have been known to be working at any one time! Although some volunteers have fallen by the wayside, we have now been joined by Jacki Pinch, Ann Jones, David Callaghan, John McCourt, Tony Martin and Julie Walker.

After nine years of coordinating the CheshireBMD project I was anxious to find a second in command and Irene agreed to take on the task of organising, indexing and checking the two sub-districts of Neston and Bebington which is now ongoing. Irene is assisted in this task with the help of the Bebington Group volunteers: Joy Keegan, June Pennell and George Highton.

It is well to remember that over the years the districts and sub-districts throughout Wirral have been the subjects of many a change, causing much confusion in the process. In 1837, when civil registration came into force, there were two districts: Birkenhead comprising two Sub-Districts of Birkenhead and Wallasey; and Wirral comprising three Sub-Districts of Neston, Woodchurch and Eastham. Since then and 1999 when it all became Wirral – there was many a reorganisation along the way, so beware!

Open Days and Help Desk

In the past, the Group has held a number of open days at Wallasey Library that proved to be very popular and although the idea of setting up a regular help desk had been explored a number of times, it didn't get off the ground until 2004 when due to the tenacity of Wendy Bennett and Irene Birch, it has now become a regular feature in the Reference Section of Wallasey Library in Earlston Road. Held on the morning of the second Friday in the month, Irene and Wendy have been assisted more recently by Paul Davies while Barbara Reid, Sheila Hamilton and I have helped on the odd occasion.

Wallasey Group also helped in the Vale Park Centenary Celebrations in 1999 when rigged out in our Victorian apparel we set up a display in Vale House. This was much appreciated by the perambulatory public and we even got to meet Queen Victoria herself who honoured the park with her presence that afternoon.

(L to R), Helen & Roger Gill and Ann Evans
at Vale Park, New Brighton during the Centenary Celebrations.

Family History Fairs

Wallasey Group has managed to make quite a name for itself, as far as dress is concerned, at the annual FHS of Cheshire's Family History Day at Northwich. For long enough we dressed up in Victorian costume until by 2006 when bored with the same old routine we went for the 1940s look. Barbara raised a few laughs with her pinny and headscarf complete with a fag hanging out of the corner of her mouth!

(L to R) Barbara Reid, Wendy Bennett, Irene Birch, Rona Ellison
and Helen & Roger Gill at Northwich, 2006.

The following year we opted for the flapper look and left a trail of feathers wherever we went! In 2008 we returned to our familiar upstairs/ downstairs formula giving Roger the opportunity of once again measuring up to the job as undertaker. Mind you, Wendy outdid the lot of us with her new generously proportioned mob-cap!

(L to R) Roger & Helen Gill, Wendy Bennett, Irene Birch and
Mike King at Northwich, 2007.

Our most flamboyant attire to date has to have been in 2009 to mark the Society's 40th Anniversary. What a wonderful way to celebrate 40 years of family history - with flowers and flares! I hasten to add at this point that we make our own costumes or trawl the local charity shops for suitable material; failing that we beg, borrow but draw the line at stealing to achieve the desired effect!

(L to R) Irene Birch, Mike King, Wendy Bennett and
Helen & Roger Gill at Northwich, 2008.

(L to R) Mike Colebourne, Helen Gill, Wendy Bennett,
Irene Birch, Mike King and Roger Gill at Northwich, 2009.

As well as Northwich, Wallasey Group has always attended the annual Family History Fair at Port Sunlight despite it usually being held the following day after Northwich, but there is always a great deal of interest at this venue. We have also put on displays at the local heritage days at Birkenhead Town Hall over the past few years although this has now come to an end since the Town Hall is currently up for sale by tender!

A new venue for the Group, in 2008, was at St. George's Hall, Liverpool, which proved very interesting, and a number of membership forms were handed out. Held at the end of the year, rather than our usual Spring Fairs, this proved to be a success and the table was booked again for 2009.

Helen M. Gill
Projects Coordinator
Wallasey Group FHSC

March 2010

Wallasey Group Leaders

Monica Hart	1990	-	1994
Anne Evans	1994	-	1995
Annie Weare	1995	-	1995
Mike King	1995	-	1997
Wendy Bennett	1997	-	2000
Wendy Bennett (Acting)	2000	-	2002
Dave Beck	2002	-	2004
Wendy Bennett (Acting)	2004	-	2008
Irene Birch	2008	-	

CHAPTER TWO

Poulton

Because of its geographical location, Wallasey was originally virtually cut off from the rest of the Wirral, by the banks of the Wallasey Pool, the treacherous Bidston Moss and the River Birket.

Initially Poulton consisted of Poulton Bridge Road, Limekiln Lane and a terrace of houses known as Hickman's Cottages, which were later incorporated into Rankin Street.

When the first Toll Bridge was built across the Wallasey Pool in 1843, to form a link with Birkenhead, it was built at Poulton, where the Pool was at its narrowest.

As a direct result, with the building of the docks and the introduction of various industries to the area, Poulton began to expand. It is noticeable that along the one main street, eventually, there were three Public Houses: The Pool Inn, The Jolly Sailor and the Eagle Arms.

Once the docks system was completed it became a hive of activity with many vessels sailing up the Pool as far as the Bidston Dock, to land their varied valuable cargoes.

The village was a popular place for the many mariners who visited from all over the world, when the prosperity of the port and docks system of the Wallasey Pool was at its height.

The Toll House

Then... The first Toll Bridge was built across the Wallasey Pool in 1843 at Poulton, where the pool was narrower, to form a link with Birkenhead. This gave the village its importance by eliminating the long journey to Moreton, to cross at the nearest bridge, should residents wish to visit Birkenhead and beyond. The Toll House was erected to serve the original wooden bridge, built by Sir Robert Vyner in 1843, when the Toll was a halfpenny. A new swing bridge was installed in 1927 and the Toll increased to 1 penny, which gave the bridge its name. The Toll was abolished in 1937 by which time it had risen to two pence.

Now... The Toll House was located just where the road curves towards the Penny Bridge. The last swing bridge was irreparably damaged some years ago and has been replaced by a very plain and practical structure. The shipping trade dwindled towards the end of the 20th century and the Bidston Dock was no longer needed, so it was drained and in-filled to reclaim the land. It has recently been offered for sale for redevelopment.

Poulton Bridge Road

Then... Poulton Bridge Road, which begins at the main crossroads, was originally quite narrow. There was only one building, on the left hand side, the original Pool Inn. On the opposite side there was a group of cottages known as The Stone Cottages or The Flags. Three faced the main road and another two were behind, set around a courtyard and accessed through an alleyway. The local midwife lived in one of the cottages. The next building was occupied for more than thirty years by Mary Whittingham, the Postmistress and grocer. Mary was there in 1891, aged 76 but by 1901 her son-in-law Peter Torrance had taken over. The last cottage further along the road was the Toll House for the Penny Bridge.[1]

Now... The Pool Inn still dominates the corner of Poulton Bridge Road, although its future is rather precarious as it has been up for sale of late. All the property on the opposite side of the road has been demolished to make way for road-widening. The length of the road to the roundabout is now dual carriageway which has meant that the foundations of the old Stone Cottages are now buried beneath the west carriageway.

[1] The painting is by Charles Hunter, the father of the late international opera diva Rita Hunter who lived at 27 Limekiln Lane.

Bird's House

Then... The old buildings on the west side of Limekiln Lane include Bird's House, built in 1697, which makes it the oldest house in Wallasey still inhabited. It is protected by a preservation order. It was the home of William Jones, the local joiner, during the second half of the 19th century. The Woosnam family, who were vergers at St. Luke's Church, have also lived there. Adjacent was a large 17th century cruck frame barn belonging to the house, which was only demolished in the 1960s.[1]

Now... Externally this house looks just as it did when it was built.

[1] This painting is another by Charles Hunter, the father of the late international opera diva Rita Hunter who lived at 27 Limekiln Lane.

Limekiln Lane

Then... The building on the right was the National School for Boys and Girls, which was opened in 1848. This building was superseded, in 1908, by a new school in Alderley Road. Later the building was converted into a Reading Room and Library for the use of local residents. It was one of four that were opened across the borough. One of the Secretaries was Mr Edmund Hopps, a member of a well know local family. The building was also occupied at some point by the Mars Firelighter Company.

Along the road from the old school was a public house, The Sailor's Return, which eventually changed its name to The Jolly Sailor.

Now... Limekiln Lane is now dominated by the huge collection of molasses tanks, the storage area for Tate & Lyle, Sugar Refiners, which have been in place for more than 60 years. The old school has been demolished and the semi-detached houses next door, numbers 18 and 20 were rebuilt in 1937 replacing the older ones.

Sadly the Jolly Sailor is no longer in existence.

Rankin Street

Then... The first new houses to be built, in the 1830s, was a row of thirteen known as Hickman's Cottages, after the builder. They were on the south side of the road at right angles to Limekiln Lane and were quite substantial. The first two were converted into a public house, The Eagle Arms, and for many years the licensee was Thomas B. Davies who, in the 1850s, was also the local grocer. Later it became known as 'Giles's' after a subsequent licensee. As more houses were required, the house building was extended eastwards and the first street completed was named Rankin Street. Hickman's Cottages then became numbers 44 to 66 Rankin Street.

Now... All the houses in Rankin Street, Portia Street, Rosalind Street etc and along Limekiln Lane towards Sherlock Lane have been demolished and a new Council housing estate was built in the 1960s. The only remaining legacy of the past is the Eagle Arms down at the bottom of Rankin Street, which looks very dilapidated and is now closed and up for sale.

Breck Road and St Luke's Church

Then... The north west corner of these crossroads is dominated by St. Luke's Church and Parish Hall. The church was opened in 1900 to cater for the growing population and is a sister church to St. Hilary's. There were a few scattered houses along this side of the road but, for the most part, it retained its rural look. It was a narrow, tree-lined country lane.

Now... St Luke's Church still dominates the north-west corner, together with the Parish Hall. The next group of houses has survived but the cottages opposite the church have all been demolished and the land now forms a car park for the Poulton Victoria Social Club.

Breck Road and Breck Place

Then... Breck Road was originally called Wallasey Road because it led to Wallasey Village. There were several small cottages on the south side and, a short distance from the crossroads, there was a group of 13 houses set down a steep incline which was named Moss View. Later the name was changed to Breck Place. At the corner, on Breck Road, was a sweet shop which, at one time, belonged to Thomas Pulford, b 1858 in Wallasey, and his wife Rebecca.

The next property in Breck Road was the Plough Inn. The pair of houses between this and Breck Place were built at a later date.

Now... Breck Road has seen many changes. Most of the old properties on the south side have disappeared. The houses in Breck Place have been replaced by a small industrial estate and the corner sweetshop is now a house, but the next two houses are still there.

The old Plough Inn building has survived having been converted into a pair of semi-detached houses.

Darley Dene and Spragg's Farm

Then... Just a little further along was 'The Slopes'. This was a large house, with extensive gardens, where John Bewley, an accountant lived. Subsequently the house was renamed 'Darley Dene' by another occupant. The house was requisitioned in WWII as a military billet and was badly damaged with much loss of life in the Blitz.

Further along Breck Road was 'Beach Cottage', almost opposite Heathbank Lodge and known locally as Spragg's Farm. Mr James Spragg, a farmer's son, b 1843 in Whitley, Cheshire, was a local milk dealer who used to deliver milk to the surrounding area using his pony and trap. He and his wife, Sarah,(nee Perkins) from Shropshire, had lived in Seacombe and came to the farm with their four children in the 1880s. The youngest, John James, carried on the business well into the 20th century, still using a pony and trap in the 1940s for his milk deliveries. It was a favourite place for local children to play in the fields and fish in 'The Triangle'.

Now... The building of the M53 Motorway, following the route of the former railway line, cut a swathe across Breck Road when a modern bridge was constructed. The road has also been widened to accommodate the increase in traffic. 'The Slopes' (Darley Dene) was demolished after the bomb damage and the site is now occupied by a builders' merchants.

Beach Cottage – Spragg's Farm – has gone and the fields belonging to the farm are now occupied by The Weatherhead Media College, a huge purpose built Senior School and the successor to Wallasey High School.

Poulton Hall and Elm Cottage

Then... Poulton Hall was an elegant, five bedroomed house which stood high up on the north east corner of the cross roads. It was surrounded by gardens and orchards and had several owners including Alfred C Hopps and his wife, Matilda Sophia, with their family. Alfred died in 1925 aged 82 and Matilda in 1927 aged 78. The hall occupied the land bordered by Mill Lane, Poulton Road and the curve of what was to become the railway line. It was put up for sale by auction in 1927.[1]

The 1875 map of the Poulton area shows that there were very few houses in Poulton Road between the Pool Inn and Somerville. There were a few cottages near to the pool Inn: Rose Cottage with the Brookes family, Alma Cottage, Madeira Cottage and Elm Cottage, which stood opposite the end of Love Lane and where Alfred Hopps' brother Edmund and his wife Miriam lived. Edmund worked in the family's oil business in Liverpool and was also Secretary of the Reading Room in Limekiln Lane.

Now... Poulton Hall was demolished in 1933 and the houses in Mill Lane, Poulton Hall Road and Roker Avenue were built on the site.

All of the original cottages have disappeared long ago and the site of Elm cottage forms part of a small 1930s housing estate. Poulton Road developed into one of the major roads of the town, stretching from Seacombe to Poulton and linking the two villages. Many houses further along the road which had been turned into shops to cater for the expanding population, have reverted to domestic use.

[1] This picture of Poulton Hall is from a painting by Harold H. Hopps.

CHAPTER THREE

Seacombe

The Village is located on the West Bank of the River Mersey and to the North of Wallasey Pool. The ferry crossing from Seacombe to Liverpool is recorded in the Domesday Book of 1086. The present ferry approach road is built on land reclaimed from the river.

The Village originated within the area close to the ferry. Industrial development spread from Birkenhead in the mid-19th Century across the Wallasey Pool. Smalt works, Seacombe Pottery, Cement Works, Iron Foundries and Shipbuilding Yards were among those industries that brought prosperity and increased population to the area. This resulted in the building of many terraces of houses north of the ferry.

Naturally the demand for goods and services increased and shopping areas developed in Brighton Street and Victoria Road (now Borough Road). There was a Cottage Hospital in Demesne Street and several Mission Houses. There was also a proliferation of public houses and beerhouses to cater for the social needs of the residents.

Poulton Road

Then... This cinema in Poulton Road was the first purpose-built one in Wallasey and opened in 1911. It was small compared to later cinemas, but was very attractive architecturally. It closed in 1959 and was converted to a supermarket.

Poulton Road was dominated by Lloyds Corner, known as such because the Lloyd family ran a bakery and also a furniture store, complete with a pawnbroker's business. As the area became more popular many of the houses had their ground floors turned into shops.

Now... Since the supermarket closed the building has remained empty and dilapidated.

Although the buildings are recognisable the area is not the busy place it once was.

Liscard Road

Then... This building was an elegant, white stone church built in Liscard Road opposite the top of Brougham Road. It catered for the needs of local Welsh Presbyterians and remained open until 1964.

At number 6 Liscard Road stood Orrell Cottage, a white painted house with a long front garden. It was situated at the corner of Albermarle Road. One of the occupants was Thomas Calderbank, a local plumber.

This pictures shows some of the 'Prefabs' that were erected in the late 1940s to replace houses that had been bombed in the Blitz. They could be erected quickly as all that was required was a suitable concrete base. Everything else arrived by lorry and was erected with ease. The whole piece of land from the Welsh Presbyterian Church in Liscard Road to the few semi-detached houses on the east side of Mainwaring Road was covered with prefabs.

Now... When the church was demolished Seacombe Library was built on the site.

The cottage was occupied by the 8th Wallasey Boy Scout Group for many years. Eventually it was demolished and a purpose-built Scout hut built in the garden which is still in regular use.

The prefab site now has a Tesco Extra store and newly built office accommodation

Myrtle Cottage

Then... This was the home of Dr. Byerley, b 1814 on the Isle of Wight, who was the 1st Poor Law Medical Officer for Health in Wallasey in 1873. When Byerley Street was built in the 1870s it was named in his honour. The cottage was demolished to make way for Jubilee Grove, no doubt celebrating Queen Victoria's Golden Jubilee.

Now... The shops that were built between Jubilee Grove and Byerley Street were badly blitzed and new modern houses now occupy the site.

Hope House

Then... This house was built prior to 1861, and was originally called Hope Cottage. The last owner was the widow of George Hulse, a Liverpool Turtle merchant. He was also the owner of North Meade House, which stood on the site of the present Town Hall. The house was demolished in 1899 and The Irving Theatre was built on the site. Following many name changes, it ultimately became the Embassy until it closed as a cinema in 1959.

Now... The Embassy is one of the few old buildings that remain in Borough Road. It is still operating as the Embassy Bingo Club.

Borough Road

Then... This part of Borough Road was bombed during WWII and the shops on the left hand side were never rebuilt. The buildings on the right hand side were all restored after the Blitz.

Now... This is the last part of the Borough Road redevelopment. The new flats on the right hand side have just been completed.

Concertina Cottages

Then... This was a housing scheme, designed and built by John Ellis, in the 1870s. His vision of building an estate of houses came to fruition on land next to the Catholic Church in Wheatland Lane. Thirty-three dwellings in six blocks were erected from the planned ninety-two. They were hexagonal in shape, as the group of six radiated from a central chimney, and, hence, became known as Concertina Cottages.

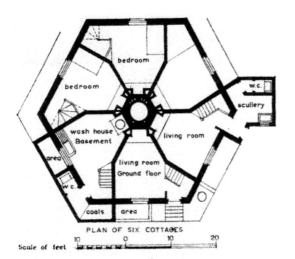

PLAN OF SIX COTTAGES

Scale of feet

Now... Concertina cottages survived until 1954 when they were all demolished. The whole area is now St. Joseph's Primary School.

Seacombe Pottery

Then... The Pottery was founded in the early 1850s by John Goodwin of Longton, Staffordshire. John Goodwin and some of his managers lived in the row of houses in Wheatland Lane, next to the Great Float Hotel. The pottery was situated on the west side of Kelvin Road and was conspicuous by the row of 6 kilns, the first of which was fired in 1852.

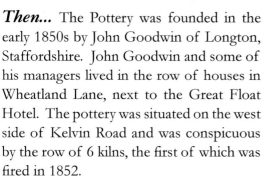

It produced mainly blue and white transfer printed earthenware. Most of its output was destined for the Canadian market. The Pottery closed in 1873 when a large uninsured consignment was lost at sea.

Now... The pottery site is now a small industrial park. There is still one original building left, Scotia House, named by the dried food packaging company which occupied the site for some years. The houses to the right of the Great Float Hotel have all been demolished.

West Seacombe Terrace

Then... This row of 24 houses, built prior to 1835, was originally named Bidston View, simply because you could see across the pottery fields to Bidston Hill. The houses were very popular with local merchants and businessmen. One side of the Terrace was eventually re-named Percy Road. No. 15 was occupied by the Hopps family. Alfred Hopps was the manager of the nearby Smalt Works, and his three sons married Dr. Byerley's three youngest daughters.

Now... Under the clearance programme in the 1960s all of the houses were demolished to make way for Council housing.

New Street

Then... This was one of the earliest houses in New Street and, in 1841, was rented by John Ball and is recorded as a house, school and yard. It was, at one time, Seacombe House Boarding School run by Mr William Giles. It eventually became numbers 1 & 2 Fern Villas and survived until 2003.

South Seacombe Villas was at the corner of Bridle Road and New Street. It was built before 1835 and was originally two residences. Eventually it became the New Street Clinic, part of the local Health and Welfare Department. At the top end of New Street was a terrace of nine houses named South Seacombe Terrace. The houses were bombed in WWII and not rebuilt. The site was used as a centre for the Local School Meals Service.

Now... All the old property on the south side at the top end of New Street has been demolished and left as a grassy open space. This gives a clear view towards Wheatland Lane, and the landmarks of the Great Float and Mona Castle hotels.

Wheatland House and Bee Hotel

Then... Wheatland Lane began at Birkenhead Road , with the Bee Hotel on one corner, and Brougham Terrace at the opposite corner. Wheatland House was an old thatched cottage next to the Bee Hotel, which was home to Philip Wilson who married the daughter of Thomas Meols of Wallasey Hall.

Now... There has been a good deal of redevelopment of Wheatland Lane. Wheatland House has been replaced by a terrace of 6 houses. However the Bee Hotel building has survived.

Birkenhead Road

Then... This area was where the original shoreline reached before the land was reclaimed to construct the ferry approach. It was where the old cottages and the Marine Hotel stood for many years until the area was redeveloped.

Now... There have been several alterations to this area and the post-war flats have been replaced with houses. The area has been generally improved by the addition of the Space Port family attraction.

Seacombe Ferry

Then... There is no documented proof of the original site of the Ferry, but it was first mentioned in the 16th Century. Originally the shoreline was much further inland, forming a small cove. In the late 19th Century a large tract of land was reclaimed and the Ferry approaches as we know them to-day were constructed. The reclaimed land was used, firstly, as a terminus for horse-drawn cabs and coaches, and then for trams and buses.

Now... The current Ferry service operates a triangular service between Seacombe, Birkenhead-Woodside and Liverpool. The present refurbished ferry building boasts a modern booking hall, café, a children's adventure playground and a sheltered waterside waiting room. Some buses still operate from the terminal, but very few compared to 50 years ago.

Ferry View Road

Then... Originally Ferry View Road began at the Promenade and finished at Mersey Street. It was not extended to Demesne Street until the Priory estate was built.

Mersey View was a row of five elegant houses which were built along the promenade at Seacombe, with a fine view across the River Mersey.

Now... Ferry View Road is now just a footpath. The left hand side is dominated by the Ventilation Station for the Mersey Tunnel. There is just a grassy bank where the houses once stood.

Stokes Ferry Hotel

Then... Records show that the earliest hotel was built on land owned by Mr Richard Smith, who leased both the hotel and ferry to Mr Thomas Parry, who ran the very successful Parry's Seacombe hotel for many years. By 1861, the licence had passed to John Stokes who hailed from Bobbington, Shropshire. He introduced American Bowls and other attractions for the many visitors from Liverpool. The gardens were laid out as pleasure grounds. Stokes Hotel was demolished by 1890 and the new Seacombe Ferry Hotel was constructed, closer to the river. The new hotel was a large imposing building with decorative brickwork.

Now... The hotel fell into decline as clientèle dwindled and the building was demolished in the 1970s 1960s. A much smaller replacement hotel, non-residential, was erected on the same site.

The Marine Hotel

Then... This hotel was originally two fishermen's cottages close to the river bank. The Marine was a very popular pub and survived for 200 years. A new larger building was eventually erected, and became No. 1 Birkenhead Road.

Now... The Marine Hotel was closed and demolished in 1992 to make way for road improvements.

Seacombe Station

Then... The railway station at Seacombe Ferry was originally for the steam train service that crossed the Wirral. The station was closed in the 1960s and the line lay derelict for several years, until plans for a second Mersey Tunnel were passed.

Now.. The route of the rail line, as far as Bidston Moss, was utilised to link the new Mersey Tunnel, opened in 1971, with the new M53 motorway.

Mersey Street and Bank House

Then.... This house was situated at the corner of Mersey Street and Victoria Road (Borough Road), close to the Seacombe Hotel. The earliest mention appears to be in 1871 when it was called 'Green Bank' and occupied by John Andrews, a wine and spirit merchant.

Mersey Street was developed prior to the 1830s and extended from close to the Seacombe Hotel, northwards. Most of the Seacombe Pottery workers settled in this area. The quality of housing was not very good and the area became very cramped. Many of the groups of houses were named – Mersey Bank Cottages, Hygeia Cottages, The Priory, Lowry Bank, High Seacombe and Mersey Terrace.

Now... The approximate site of Bank House is now occupied by Victoria House, a multi-storey block of flats.

The whole of Mersey Street has been cleared, except for one property. When the old properties were cleared away, the Priory council housing estate replaced it.

Catherine Terrace and Mersey House

Then... This was a terrace of three houses, whose resident families remained constant from the mid 1800s until 1911, except for one change at No.1. Antonio Longobardo, a foreign correspondent, lived at Number 2 with his family as late as 1911.

This old detached house was known as Mersey House and in 1861 it was a school run by Miss Mary S G McLeod, a teacher, and her sisters. It was occupied by various people until the time of WWI, and then it was left empty for some years. Eventually it was demolished and the local Labour Exchange was built. This was in use until the regeneration of Liscard, when Dominick House was built.

Now... The terrace was demolished when the Priory housing estate was built in the 1930s.

The Labour Exchange building has survived and has been upgraded, to be used for the benefit of the community.

Demesne Street

Then... Demesne Street was very busy, as one of the main streets of Seacombe. It was mainly residential, with the ubiquitous corner shops and public houses. It extended from the junction with Borough Road to the Guinea Gap. There were several styles of houses, varying from small terraces to large Victorian houses with attics and cellars. The Cottage Hospital was at number 53.

Now... The only legacy of the original Demesne Street is the name. As part of a huge area of regeneration, most of the properties have been demolished, the side streets have disappeared and new council housing has replaced them. Now, there is no through road to Guinea Gap. As this book is being prepared even more of the 1960s properties are being demolished.

Demesne Street

Then... The tram lines being laid were extending the track to Guinea Gap.

Now... This part of Demesne Street now stops at Toronto Street.

Borough Road

Then... Victoria Road was one of the four original roads of Poulton-cum-Seacombe, and became the main shopping area for the small village of Seacombe. The fire brigade requested a change of name to avoid confusion with Victoria Road, New Brighton. The road was re-named Borough Road in 1918.

Now... Almost the whole area, including the south side of Borough Road, has been cleared of all the 19th Century houses and shops, and has been replaced with a Council built housing estate. The only original building remaining is on the left hand corner.

Borough Road and Church Road

Then... The bank building which dominated the corner of Borough Road and Brighton Street also housed a local estate agent and other offices. It became a restaurant but was eventually closed.

The Seacombe Presbyterian Church at the south corner of Belle Vue Road which was opened in 1865 and demolished prior to 1960. Next door was the Wallasey Printers, the proprietors of the Wallasey News.

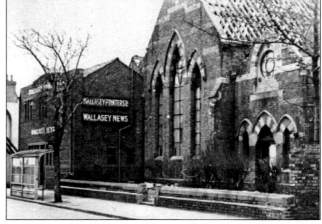

Now... The bank has been demolished and the site has remained empty. Because some of the surrounding land is being regenerated hopefully this plot will be included.

The Presbyterian church and the Wallasey News building have disappeared and a purpose-built supermarket with its large car park has replaced them.

Brighton Street

Then... Brighton Street was the busiest part of Seacombe, teeming with shops of all descriptions and a constant hive of activity. On the corner of Vienna Street was a furniture store, owned by Emanuel Kopetsky, who was born in Bohemia. The store was converted into a working men's club, called 'The Vienna Hall'. The building was later demolished and the Marina Cinema replaced it.

The Marina Cinema opened in 1916 and was in constant use, progressing from silent films to 'talkies' during its lifetime.

Now... Most of the side roads have disappeared or have been revamped with modern housing. Sad to say, but some of these modern houses have just been demolished and the outcome of any further redevelopment is awaited.

The Marina Cinema closed in 1956 and the building just left to decay. It was demolished in the 1970s along with the surrounding properties. It is now part of the grounds of Riverside Primary School.

Beaufort Terrace

Then... This row of elegant houses on the east side of Brighton Street stretched from Brougham Road to North Meade House. Eventually several of these houses were converted into shops but, those that remained, housed, at various times, a doctor's surgery, a dentist and an optician among others. North Meade was eventually purchased by the Council, demolished, and the present Town Hall erected in 1914.

Now... As soon as the new Town Hall was completed in 1914, it was requisitioned as a military hospital during WWI. It was officially opened as the Town Hall by the Mayor, Alderman E G Parkinson, in 1920. The houses and shops of Beaufort Terrace were demolished in the 1960s to make way for Council offices. The row of houses to the north of the Town Hall had also been demolished for the same purpose. The buildings are known as the North and South Annexe.

The Sessions House

Then... In the mid-19th Century, the nearest gaol was in Birkenhead, so any felons had to be kept overnight in the local constable's house. Therefore, Sessions House, complete with cells, was built in Liscard Road, between Falkland Road and Clarendon Road. The building was converted into a cinema in 1914 and opened as the Old Court House. Several name changes later, it finally became the Continental, showing a wide range of continental films. It closed as a cinema in 1963, reopened as a Bingo Hall, but this venture did not survive for long.

Now... The building was left empty for many years and eventually demolished. A new block of flats has just been built on the site and is presently awaiting occupants.

CHAPTER FOUR

Egremont

Egremont is situated adjacent to the River Mersey and links Seacombe and New Brighton. The area spread as the ferry crossing service to Liverpool developed, with the purchase of the ferry buildings by Captain John Askew in 1829. The ferry service ended when the pier was badly damaged as a ship collided with it in 1941 and it was eventually demolished.

The main street was Barn Lane, which was eventually renamed King Street, after Ellen King who owned land in the vicinity. The Egremont Hotel in Tobin Street later became the Egremont Institute which was used for church services, concerts, evening classes and other educational activities. The building lay empty for many years and was finally demolished.

As with Seacombe, the increase in population gave way to the building of many terraces of small houses, to accommodate the local workforce. These were mainly to the west side of King Street.

Houses at the east end of Church Street and its side streets, Charles Street, Church Avenue and John Street were so badly damaged in the WWII blitz that they were never rebuilt. It was a scene of devastation until new council housing was built to replace them.

Brighton Street

Then... These shops on Brighton Street were between Falkland Road and Church Street. Priestley's Photographic Studio was located at No. 1 Falkland Road.

The Egremont Town Hall stood at the south corner of Church Street, together with the Council Offices, until the new Town Hall replaced it after WWI. The move was delayed because the new building was requisitioned as a military hospital until after the war was over.

Now... The photographic studios are no more and the house is now a residential home. The row of shops has been replaced with modern housing. Egremont Town Hall was demolished many years ago.

Tobin Street

Then... When Egremont was first developed the only shops built were in Tobin Street. There was a dairy, grocer, stationer, hairdresser, confectioner, refreshment rooms and tobacconist at various times, as well as the ferry, the pier and the hotel. The shops lined the south side of the street and stretched down as far as the ferry. The rest of the area was residential.

Now... All that is left on Tobin Street are the new houses of 'Newlands' sheltered housing development. The area where the ferry terminal once stood is now a car park and the Egremont Ferry Hotel is an enlarged and modernised public house.

Egremont Ferry and Promenade

Then... The photograph shows the Egremont Ferry building. A regular service ran from here to Liverpool until the pier was damaged in 1941.

Egremont Promenade was very popular for people to stroll along to take the sea air and visit New Brighton Tower.

Now... Egremont Ferry closed in 1941 after the pier was damaged. The area is now a car park.

Egremont Promenade is still a popular place for walkers, joggers and fishermen.

Charter House

Then... Charter House was the first multi-storey block of flats and was built in 1960 to celebrate the 50th anniversary of the granting of Borough status to Wallasey.

Church Street was one of the first roads to be built, leading from the Egremont Ferry, after Sir John Tobin had purchased the land for building St John's church. His son, also John, was the first incumbent of the church in 1833. The vicarage stood at number 43, next to Egremont Primary School.

Now... Charter House is still occupied but has recently been earmarked for demolition.

Much of Church Street was very severely bombed during WWII, leaving large swathes of rubble. The vicarage and some of the adjoining houses were bombed. Eventually there was a huge rebuilding programme and now the devastated area has been restored with Council housing.

Gothic House and Littler's Terrace

Then... The large detached house at the top of Church Street, on the south side, became known as the 'Gothic House'.

Littler's Terrace was built between the Gothic House at the end of Church Street and the King's Arms pub in Liscard Road.

Now... Although much in the area has changed, Littler's Terrace still stands. However, the Gothic House was demolished before the war.

Liscard Hall

Then... Liscard Hall was the home of Sir John Tobin and was built in what is now Central Park. It was built before 1835 and, when Sir John died in 1851, he was succeeded at the Hall by his son-in-law, Harold Littledale, who owned Liscard Model Farm. When Mr Littledale died in 1889, the house and grounds were bought by the Wallasey Local Board and opened to the public as Central Park. The house became the School of Art and was used by thousands of students over the years, but became empty due to progressive changes in the local education system.

Now... In 2008 there was a huge fire at the empty Liscard Hall. After the fire, the building was judged to be structurally dangerous and was reduced to a pile of rubble immediately. The latest news is that the area will probably be landscaped rather than the Hall being re-built.

King Street

Then... The old building at the corner of Trafalgar Road was originally the Egremont Presbyterian Church which opened after 1862. The first minister was Robert Cameron. A new church was built at the corner of Manor Road in 1907 and the old building became the Lyceum Cinema. In 1933 the building was reconstructed replacing the classical Greek design of the original church with restrained classical 1930s designs. It first opened as the Gaumont Palace, later changed to the Classic and then the Unit Four, to reflect the changing formats in cinema-going. In its last period it was divided into 6 screens.

Now... The cinema closed and after being empty for some years was demolished. A new block of luxury apartments has now been built on the site and was completed in 2009.

Stringhey Road

Then... Stringhey Road connects Trafalgar Road with Manor Road and has always been a mixture of shops and houses. The main row of shops, on the east side, ran from Marsden Road to Greenwood Lane and there was quite a variety to choose from. Kerr's the grocer, Litherland's hardware and Whitfield's dairy were just a few.

Now... All the shops from Marsden Road to Greenwood Lane have been demolished and a row of new houses has been built during 2009. As this book is nearing completion the houses are finished but awaiting occupation.

Trafalgar Road

Then... Originally the site was occupied by Vernon's School. when the road was known as Abbot's Lane. Threlfall's Hygienic Creamery was erected in place of the school. This eventually became Hanson's Dairy at 76 Trafalgar Road which was also used as a depot for local milk deliveries, when milk was delivered daily to your door.

Now... The dairy building has survived but has been converted into flats. The shop windows have been bricked up but parts of the frieze above the ground floor remain, telling the details of previous occupants.

Manor House and Cliff House

Then... This house, originally called 'Seabank', stood at the lower end of Manor Lane and was the home of the Penkett family for many years. When John Penkett died, the property was inherited by his daughter, Mrs Mary Anne Maddock. On her death, in 1888, it was acquired by the Mercantile Marine Service Association and used to extend the area of Mariner's Park. The house was used as an infirmary for residents until it was demolished and replaced by the John Davies Memorial Infirmary in 1937.

Cliff House was built with money given by William Cliff in memory of his daughter, Rosa Webster. It was built to accommodate retired and poor mariners and provided them with somewhere comfortable to live and socialise. The house was closed in 1977 and was eventually demolished.

Now... The John Davies Memorial Infirmary was demolished in 2003 as part of an ongoing development and has been replaced by the current Care Home. The area where the Manor House stood is used as a well-kept bowling green for the present residents, complete with a summer house for spectators.

A two-storey, purpose-built Care Home now stands in the area once occupied by Cliff House. It offers accommodation and care facilities for 32 residents, in single rooms. The houses and bungalows that form Mariners' Park have always been well-maintained and, during the past 127 years, almost all of the original buildings have been replaced by higher quality accommodation.

Mother Redcap's

Then... Much has been written about the history of this original old house which stood on Egremont Promenade between Caithness Drive and Lincoln Drive. It was built in 1595 and had several name changes during its lifetime and many fanciful stories have been written about it. One such owner, a Mr Kitchingman, is credited with the responsibility for prohibiting vehicular traffic along the promenade from Seacombe to New Brighton. The Council needed the land in front of the house in order to build the promenade and Mr Kitchingman would only give the land on condition that no carriages should be allowed to use the promenade. The house was used in later years as a café but, when left empty, fell into disrepair.

Now... The original building no longer exists. The house was eventually ravaged by fire. The current replacement is a complex of accommodation for the elderly, offering residential and nursing care in comfortable, modern surroundings, which was opened in 1988.

CHAPTER FIVE

New Brighton and Upper Brighton

Prior to 1830, New Brighton didn't exist. The area to the east of Mount Road, and north of Mount Pleasant Road and Magazine Lane was just a mass of rocky outcrops, heathland and sandhills with a few dwellings and was known as Rock Point.

It was in 1830 that James Atherton, a wealthy, retired merchant from Liverpool, purchased 170 acres of this barren land. He had a dream to create a healthy seaside resort to rival the south coast town of Brighton. Thus New Brighton and Upper Brighton were born.

He drew up plans for new roads, rising in tiers, from the point that became the bottom of Victoria Road, along the coast as far as the rocks known as the Red Noses.

His vision was to have the roads set out in a grid system, rising from the lowest level, so that, when the fine houses he proposed to build were finished, every resident would have an uninterrupted view across Liverpool Bay.

New Brighton Bathing Pool

New Brighton Bathing Pool, an Art Deco styled building, was opened in 1934. There were shops each side of the façade, with dual entrances for both the promenade and inside of the pool. At the time, it was the largest open air pool in the world and was a very popular place to swim during the summer months. During the 1950s an annual Bathing Beauty contest was held, which gave New Brighton the benefit of national publicity. However, as the popularity of the resort dwindled, the pool was closed and left to decay. The storms of 1990 breeched the sea wall in several places and caused irreparable damage to the structure of the pool and it had to be demolished. The site has lain empty since demolition. The good news is that work has now commenced on the redevelopment of the site.

Victoria Road

Then... So much has been written about this part of the promenade that only a brief mention should be necessary. At the bottom of Victoria Road, on the seafront, was Aquarium Parade also known as Teapot Row and subsequently the Ham and Egg Parade. It was a two-storey row of shops and eating houses that became notorious for its bawdiness and, in 1905, it was bought by the Council and demolished. Victoria Gardens replaced it as a pleasant place for locals and visitors to relax. The gardens were opened in 1913 and included the first open-air Floral Pavilion Theatre.

Now... Once again the area has been cleared for the new Floral Pavilion to be built. As part of the current regeneration programme taking place in New Brighton, there are plans to build more luxury apartments on the land which extends from the promenade to Virginia Road.

New Brighton Piers

Then... New Brighton actually had two piers, built side by side. First of all a pier was required to allow access to and from the ferry boats that plied their trade between New Brighton and Liverpool. The Council bought the pier in 1928 and it was then reconstructed to a modern design. The second part, known as the Promenade Pier, was purely to cater for the entertainment of visitors. There was a bandstand, a dance area, various stalls and a restaurant and bar.

Now... Due to falling visitor numbers, and the decline in other facilities at New Brighton, the ferry service became uneconomical to run and the Liverpool to New Brighton service was discontinued. In 1973 the piers were dismantled and all that is left is the area where the entrances had been.

The Tivoli Theatre

Then... The Tivoli Theatre stood on the Tower Promenade between Tollemache Street and Egerton Street and was a very popular venue for live variety shows. It opened in 1914 and there was a row of shops at the front with Reece's Tivoli Cafe on the first floor. For a few brief periods the theatre was converted, unsuccessfully, into a cinema, so it reverted to variety shows and revues. It lasted until 1955 when the ground floor briefly became an amusement arcade. The building was badly damaged by fire in 1976 and was demolished.

Now... This site has now been redeveloped with a complex of modern apartments.

Tower and Football Grounds

Then... The main focal point of the Tower Grounds was the Tower which was completed in 1900. It stood above the ornate brick building which housed the Tower Ballroom and Theatre and was 562 feet high,(621 feet above sea level), and was taller than the Eiffel Tower. The structure was neglected during WWI and became unsafe so it was dismantled between 1919 and 1921. The ballroom and theatre were preserved and the building housed a menagerie for some years. There was a football, athletics stadium and cycle track within the grounds and New Brighton Football Club played there for several seasons. The stadium was also used for Stock Car Racing in the 1970s.

There was a devastating fire on 5th April 1969 and the whole building was gutted. Nothing could be saved and it was demolished.

Now... Sadly, all of this has disappeared. The decay came in the 1950s and 60s. The fire was the last straw and the Tower and Grounds just died. The area of the football ground is a new housing development.

The Palace Theatre

Then... The Palace Theatre on the Marine Promenade opened in the early 1880s and was gradually expanded to include Salt Water Baths, a Concert Hall and Variety Theatre. The name was changed to the Palace and Pavilion Theatre and it became a nationally acclaimed venue. The building of the Tower had an adverse effect but the Palace did survive until 1913. In that year it was sold and became the Gaiety Theatre.

Now... The present Palace is a covered Amusement Arcade on the Marine Promenade. It is an Art Deco building which has been redecorated recently to blend in with the new Floral Pavilion facade.

Marine Promenade

Then... Stretching from Rowson Street along the promenade towards the Palace, this parade of buildings was home to some of the resort's most prestigious hotels - The Queens Royal, The Grand and the Marine. Union Terrace was a row of Victorian houses that were either private residences or boarding houses offering holiday accommodation when the resort was at its height of popularity.

Now... The houses from Waterloo Road towards the Palace now have shops at ground level, including a café and fish and chip shop. The Queen's Royal Hotel is still a restaurant but the Grand Hotel has been demolished. The rest of the block, to Rowson Street, now houses restaurants, clubs and bars.

Alexandra Hall and Wintergardens Theatre

Then... The Alexandra Hall, opened in 1907 at the corner of Atherton Street and Alexandra Road as a theatre and evolved in 1931 into the Winter Gardens Theatre. It began to show films in 1936 and finally closed in 1957 but briefly re-opened as a Bingo Hall in the 1960s.

Now... Purpose-built sheltered housing has been built on the site.

Victoria Road

Then... The Trocadero Cinema was opened in Victoria Road in 1922 and was advertised as the latest in cinema development. It even had its own orchestra. Eventually it was adapted for 'talkies' in 1930. The cinema survived until 1956 when it re-opened as a supermarket.

There was a Woolworth's store at 71-73 Victoria Road, between Albert Street and Mason Street and, along with hundreds of their other stores, it was very popular. This photograph has been included because there are now no Woolworth's stores in existence since the company ceased trading on the high street.

Now... Along with the other old buildings at the lower end of Victoria Road, the premises that had housed the Trocadero succumbed to the march of the bulldozers. The redeveloped part of the road is now named Victoria Parade.

The Woolworths store was also within the clearance area of Victoria Road and has been replaced by modern housing.

The Convalescent Home

Then... The Convalescent Home for Women and Children opened in Rowson Street in the mid-nineteenth century and very much later, in 1924, it became the Maris Stella Roman Catholic High School for Girls.

Now... When Maris Stella school closed, the buildings were demolished and a new purpose-built complex of sheltered accommodation for the elderly was built on the site.

SS. Peter and Paul's Church

Then... The church at the corner of Hope Street and Rowson Street was opened in 1881 as SS. Peter and Paul and was used until the new church was built in Atherton Street in 1935. The old church was eventually demolished.

Long before SS Peter and Paul was built in Atherton Street the plot of land had a previous history. The original house, built in 1847, was called Sandrock and in 1851 was occupied by James Stringer, and his family. Sometime in the early 20th century it was bought by an order of Roman Catholic nuns and became the Convent of the Cenacle. In 1915 it became a Red Cross military hospital. After WWI the house became empty and was bought by the Roman Catholic Church.

Now... The site of the old SS Peter & Paul's Church is now a delivery area for the Somerfield supermarket.

The church was closed in 2008, due to a dwindling congregation and remains empty. At the present time its future is uncertain, although there is an active group who are campaigning for it to be saved.

Ewart House

Then... This large detached house stood near the corner of Wellington Road and Portland Street. It was the home of James Atherton, the retired merchant who was the force behind the development of New Brighton. When he died in 1838, his widow sold the property to Mr Joseph Christopher Ewart who named it Ewart House. It had several owners over the years and was finally demolished in about 1937.

Now... Ewart House was replaced by a block of luxury flats named Portland Court. The building still survives and is a desirable place to live, with its wonderful views over Liverpool Bay.

Hotel Victoria

Then... This landmark building at the corner of Albion Street and Portland Street has dominated the skyline since it was first erected. It was a residential hotel and also a popular meeting place. Eventually the Assembly Rooms next door were acquired and the hotel was extended to include a ballroom. It became a prestigious venue for dinners, dances, wedding receptions and various types of entertainment, including Jazz and Country and Western evenings.

Now... The Hotel Victoria closed and was demolished in 2006. At the present time there is an ongoing project building luxury apartments on the site.

Rowson Street

Then... The Sandrock Hotel stood at the top of Molyneux Drive and Rowson Street. As New Brighton's popularity declined, the Hotel closed and it was used as auction rooms and a storage facility. Eventually the building was abandoned and fell into disrepair.

Now... In recent years the building was demolished and replaced by a complex of luxury accommodation, known as 'Roberts Homes'.

Central School

Then... The building at the corner of the south side of Field Road was the Wallasey Technical School which opened in 1889 to offer technical and manual instruction at senior level. After reorganisation, the school became the annexe to the new school built in Coronation Avenue. The Field Road School was used as the Commercial Department, offering bookkeeping, shorthand and typing to senior girls. When it was no longer required it was used by the Wirral College of Art.

Now.... The school was demolished and new purpose-built flats are now on the site.

Field Road

Then... Field Road was the original Tramcar Terminus and Depot for New Brighton. The tram sheds were situated on the north side of the road, just past Busby Cottages. The first track had been laid in 1879 to provide a link with Seacombe Ferry. As demand increased the service was expanded until the trams were replaced with buses in 1929 and the sheds were used as garages for them.

Now... The old garages have been demolished and a row of new houses now occupies the site.

St. James' School and Liscard Chapel

Then... This building in Magazine Lane was originally St James' C of E School and was opened in 1847 to cater for the needs of children of New Brighton. It was affiliated to the parish church of St James in Victoria Road and was also known as Rock School. It continued to be used until some classes were relocated to Egerton Street, next to the Methodist Church. Both sites were used until the late 1930s when pupils from here were transferred to Vaughan Road.

Liscard chapel was built in 1842 and paid for by John Astley Marsden of "Liscard Castle", costing £1,000. The building was bombed in WWII and was restored but what had been the school hall, at the side, was damaged beyond repair and a new Parish Hall was built in 1953-4.

Now... The old school building has been used as a nightclub for many years and has changed hands several times, becoming known locally as 'The Tavern'.

The church was closed in 1972 and was eventually demolished. Marsden Court, a sheltered housing development for the elderly now occupies the site. The Parish Hall that was built in 1953-4 is still in constant use for the benefit of the local community.

Albert Terrace

Then... Albert Terrace was a small court of houses off the south side of Mount Pleasant Road, opposite the Quarry Bowling Green. In 1881 it is recorded as Albert Place on the census. It was typical of the old 'court' type of accommodation to be seen in other parts of the town, with a communal pump, midden and privy and was paved with large flagstones. There were six houses in the court and, in 1891, Alfred Tushingham's greengrocer's shop was on one corner and John Varty's Plough Inn was on the other.

Now... Albert Terrace became uninhabitable due to its age, and was eventually demolished. A block of new flats now covers the site.

The Telegraph Inn and Mount Pleasant Road

Then... The Telegraph Inn is a very old established pub, which was known locally as Annie Todd's.

Now... The Telegraph Inn is still a busy pub and has been extended as its popularity has increased.

Coronation Avenue

Then... The Wallasey Secondary Technical School was built in Coronation Avenue in 1938, offering technical education for boys and girls. The boys' department was on the ground floor and the girls' department on the first floor. Everything was kept separate except for a shared gymnasium. By 1960 the boys had moved to Mosslands Drive and the girls to Oxley Avenue in Leasowe and the building became Quarrymount School for Girls.

Now... When the school was closed, it was demolished and the site, combined with the surrounding clearance area, has now become a small housing estate.

CHAPTER SIX

Liscard

In 1811 the total population of Liscard was 289 composed of 54 families living in 51 houses. 40 from the 54 had their living from agriculture and 7 in trade.

Most lived in the Wallasey Road, Seaview Road, Rake Lane and Liscard Road area. The houses were built mainly of sandstone quarried from Liscard Common at the junction of Rake Lane, Upper Rowson Street and Magazine Lane. There were a few brick built as well.

Wallasey High School

Then... Wallasey High School opened in 1883 in the Liscard Concert Hall in Manor Road. The school in Mount Pleasant Road was completed in 1908 but didn't actually open until 1909. With the re-organistion of Secondary Education in the 1970s, the name was changed to Weatherhead High School.

Now... As numbers and sites of Weatherhead increased it was decided to build a new school, in Breck Road, which would accommodate all pupils on one site. The old school was demolished and the site used for Mount Primary School and New Brighton Children's Centre.

Liscard Castle

Then... John Astley Marsden, a brush manufacturer from Liverpool, built Liscard Castle in 1810. On the 1841 tithe map it is called Marine Villa. As it had turrets and above the main bay window stood a lion, it became known as Liscard Castle or Brush Castle. Mr Marsden paid for the Liscard Independent Chapel in Princess Road to be built. The house was eventually divided into 3 parts in an endeavour to sell it – the Turrets, the Tower and the Castle. It gradually fell into decay and was demolished in 1902. Turret Road and Castle Road are reminders of where it stood.

Now... As Liscard Castle fell into disrepair it was demolished to make way for many houses to be built. The turrets on the houses at the corners of Turret and Castle Road pay homage to the interesting building which once graced this site.

Seaview Road

Then.... The Liscard Palace Cinema was opened in Seaview Road in 1911 and was originally called the Liscard Electric Palace. It had seating capacity of 700 and two shops were incorporated into the frontage. Over the years, a few alterations were made including rebuilding the front after removing all the elaborate plaster work and replacing it with brick. It eventually closed in 1959.

Seaview Road was originally a country lane known as Marsden's Lane as it led from Liscard towards Liscard Castle owned by John Marsden and stopped at a gate at Hoseside Road. The buildings shown in the right hand corner are the cottage and stables run by the Gibbons family.

Now... After the demise of the once thriving Liscard Palace cinema the building was refurbished and opened by Lennon's supermarket. It is the Shoemarket at the present time.

The buildings on the left hand side of the road still remain although there has been many changes of occupancy. The right hand side has been completely modernised over the years.

Wellington Hotel

Then... The old Wellington Hotel was built possibly earlier than 1850 when locals would meet around an 'L' shaped bar. In 1898 the bar was run by William Price and in 1902 by William Davies. The site to the side of it was purchased and the new Wellington was opened in 1937, when the old one was demolished for road widening. In the late 1960s the manager was Bert Lloynds whose son-in-law, Brian Waight was the manager of the Royal Ferry Hotel in New Brighton, later the Chelsea.

Now... The Wellington Hotel still stands proudly on its corner and now displays the name Duke's. At the extreme left of the picture is the building once a centrepiece of the planned shopping area – the Electric showrooms. This lies empty at present after being vacated by a frozen food company.

Liscard Village

Then... This photograph was taken at the corner of Liscard Road and Wallasey Road around 1900. The corner shop is Clare & Co, Victoria Mills, millers, cornflour and provision dealers. In Belvidere Terrace, where Woolworth's was to be, there was Mrs Drewe, a stationer, Jas. Hodgson, fishmonger & poulterer and John Taylor, a butcher. The corner opposite Clare & Co was developed as a bank building in 1908.

This view has changed many times over the years, having the 'monkey house' shelter, a policeman directing traffic from an island, a roundabout and the present one-way system. Constant in the view has been the distant building which was once the chemist's on the junction of Manor Road and Liscard Village

Now... This is a very different scene. The Barclay's building on the left was opened in 1908 though not as Barclay's at that time. The shops on the right have been rebuilt further back and what many remember as Burton's corner is now Lloyd's TSB. This corner has had a varied career with supermarkets such as Scott's in the late 60s being just one. Burton's however has survived round the corner with its sister shop Dorothy Perkins taking half of the floor space.

The roundabout has now been replaced with a complex one-way system and many pedestrian crossing places. In the distance can be seen the old building, once a chemist and now a take-away.

Liscard Village

Then... Gibbons' livery stables were established in the late 1800s and were run by the sons of Stephen Gibbons of the Boot Inn - William, b 1862, Harold, b 1865 and James b 1871. In 1891 William was termed livery stable manager and lived with his wife, Mary, and brother James who drove the Hackney carriages. The Gibbons' moved with the times as, by 1901, they were car proprietors.

Built on the site of Gibbons' stables, this building opened in 1926 as the Capitol Picture House seating 1,390 in its balconied interior. When it first opened there was room for an orchestra too. In those days films changed at least once a week and it was the main form of entertainment for many. In 1959 the building was modernised and re-named the ABC Cinema which only survived until 1974 when it became a Bingo Hall – until the 1990s when it closed.

Now... The sad sight of what was a thriving cinema and bingo hall in the past shows the change in interests over the years. The Capitol is boarded up at the front and demolition work is taking place at the rear.

Liscard Village

Then... Urmson's House was the last example of an 18th century property in Wallasey. It was built in 1729 by J. Urmson, a farmer, and was opposite the Fire Station in Liscard. It was demolished in 1928.

The Bon Bon at 20 Liscard Village is one shop that has been a constant over the years. In 1901 it was a confectioners and was owned by Hannah Branford, b 1849 in Great Crosby, who lived with her daughter aged 12. Although it is not named as such on the census, the early photograph tells its own story.

Now... Urmson's ivy clad house has been replaced by a row of shops, set back from Liscard Village.

The Bon Bon is now 'The Sweet Shop' but did remain the Bon Bon for many years. Although some modernisation has taken place it is still basically the same. The old lamp post has been replaced by a traffic sign.

The Fire Station

Then... The first fire appliances were kept in front of the water tower in Mill Lane and up to 1900 Wallasey Fire Brigade was run by volunteers who were paid a small retainer. The old fire station, opened in 1898, was on part of the well known site in Manor Road and consisted of stabling and a yard. There was a manual fire engine and ladders with horse sheds in Seacombe and Wallasey Village. After a serious fire at New Brighton Tower a steam fire engine was purchased and in 1914 funding was provided for the new fire station to be built plus 2 fire engines. This opened the following year.

Now... Sherlock House now occupies the site vacated when the Fire Station was demolished on its move to a new site in Mill Lane. This building houses offices for Angela Eagle the local MP, Penkett Holdings and Sherlock Homes, both property management companies and Manor Chiropody Clinic, amongst others. The extensive land has also provided a pay and display car park. The last photograph shows the new fire station in Mill Lane.

Egerton Grove

Then... Egerton cottage was three small thatched cottages joined together which were demolished in 1913.

The left-hand one at the end has had slates replacing thatch.

The first telephone exchange in Wallasey was opened between 1886 & 1893 above the chemists shop at the corner of Zig Zag Road. This was adequate at the time because there were less than 500 lines in use. A new exchange was built in 1921 and by 1922 the lines had more than tripled. The Wallasey exchange became automatic in 1964. *It is in Rake La., not Egerton Gro.*

Now... The building of the exchange still stands but, alas, due to automation, there are no smiling people manning the switch board.

On the corner of Egerton Grove stands Hebron Hall which was founded by Percy and Edward Sheldon and friends as a meeting place for the Plymouth Brethren. It is now an Hebron Evangelical Church.

On the left of Egerton Gro. is a school, built to replace the one (still standing) in Liscard Rd. It was in use as Council offices until Jan. 2019.

Queen's Arms

Then... The old Queen's Arms was on the corner of Queen Street and Liscard Village. Attached to the old pub was a farm yard where cows were milked and housed. The Wallasey Commissioners, who were replaced by the Local Board of Health in 1852, held their first meeting at the Queen's in a room above the stables.

Now... The new "Queens" was built behind the old pub allowing space for car parking at the front after the old one was demolished.

Clifton Hall and Wallasey Grammar School

NAVY LEAGUE TRAINING HOME, LISCARD, CHES. I.

Then.... Clifton Hall was a large house in Withens Lane, next to the Grammar School, and amongst the owners was Captain John Herron, who was Chairman of the Ferries Committee. After his death in 1897, the house became the Lancashire Sea-Training Home for Boys which was for poor, homeless boys between the ages of 13 and 16. It was also the local HQ of the Navy League which moved out during WWII. It became the Wallasey Technical College in 1949 and later, a campus for the Wirral Metropolitan College.

The first grammar school sited in Withens Lane was opened in 1876 and was the fourth site for Wallasey Grammar School. It bore a striking resemblance to the site in St George's Road but by the early 1900's was too small for purpose and the fifth school, which opened in 1911 was built on the land at the rear. The old school was demolished making way for the playing fields.

Now... When the Wirral Metropolitan College closed, the buildings were demolished, and a new housing estate now occupies the site.

The Grammar School site has not altered very much since the fifth school was opened in 1911. The school is now inhabited by Liscard Primary School whose Head is Mrs R. Littler. The school moved into this site when Egerton Grove School was closed and the buildings left were turned into Council offices.

Manor Road School

Then... Manor Road School was built in 1905 to accommodate the growing population of Wallasey. It became Liscard Secondary Modern in the 50s and the Withensfield School in the 60s. In the 70s Withensfield Middle School moved to the Grammar School site in Withens Lane and the old building was demolished for housing.

Now... After the school was demolished the land was set aside for building. These modern houses grace the site now.

Liscard Shops

Then... Liscard was a popular shopping centre with well known high street shops such as Marks and Spencer's and Manfield shoes and also many local traders. Marks and Spencer's closed in 1990. The gable end seen in the photograph shows the location of St Mary's School for Girls.

Beyond the shops in the photograph it can be seen that changes are being made. The shops on the corner of Liscard Road and Wallasey Road are being demolished so that they can be re-built further back, thus making the road wider.

Now... The whole of the shopping area is now pedestrianised. Sadly some of the popular high street stores have gone to be replaced by bargain retail outlets. Primark occupies the Marks & Spencer's site and B&M budget shop has filled the large gap left by the departure of Littlewoods.

The scene today does bear some resemblance to the earlier photograph. This section of Liscard Road has been pedestrianised.

The Co-op and Pear Tree Cottage

Then.... This co-operative shop was opened in 1911 in Liscard Road. It was part of the Birkenhead and District Co-operative Society and took up the whole corner of Liscard Road and Liscard Crescent. Whilst it sold food in its early days, by the 1970s it had become a department store with a cafeteria on the top floor.

Pear Tree cottage was situated on Liscard Road near a group of 9 cottages called Belvidere Terrace, which was more recently the site of Woolworth's. This photograph probably shows the rear of the cottage. In 1861 Ann Wilson, b.1806, lived there with her niece and nephew, Ruth and William Wilson. She is described as a proprietor of houses.

Now... There is now no sign of the majestic Co-op building. It has been replaced by a modern edifice housing McDonald's, Ethel Austin, Superdrug and Iceland.

Pear Tree cottage is long gone. The cottages alongside it have also met the same fate and been replaced by shops. Woolworths, in Liscard Road, was on this site for many years but recently has been replaced by Poundland.

St Mary's Boys School

Then... St Mary's National School opened in 1839 as an Elementary school under the auspices of the National Society. It was connected with St John's Church until 1864 when the building became inadequate and it transferred to St Mary's School.

Now... This site has almost gone back to its roots of education as it is now being used by Wirral Met College. Prior to that it had a varied career including being part of Max Speilmann photographers.

Victoria Central Hospital and Martin's Lane

Then... The foundation stone for the Victoria Central Hospital was laid in July 1899 and the building was opened on New Year's Day, January 1901. The hospital was a voluntary one supported by public subscription and donations until it was taken over under the National Health Act in 1948. A new extension was built in 1957 to house the outpatients department, minor operations theatre, four laboratories and the physiotherapy department. Due to the opening of Arrowe Park Hospital, it closed in 1982 and the outpatients department was moved to Mill Lane Hospital.

The old tram is seen here passing the corner of Martin's Lane, Liscard, with the Victoria Central Hospital in the background. In 1901 the first house was occupied by Margaret Rock, b 1846 in Goole, Yorkshire, and her 3 daughters. Next door to her was Joseph Sanderson LRCP, S.Edin., a physician and surgeon, b 1867 in Huyton. He lived with his father and 4 sisters. The space between the houses and Liscard Road was a fenced, grassed area.

Now... The hospital was demolished after Arrowe Park was opened in 1981 and on the front of the site is a new Ambulance Station. The outpatients' buildings and laboratories have become St George's Nursing Home, a private facility which provides care for the elderly.

The upper floors of the shops show the alterations made to the once majestic houses. The fenced, grassed area is no longer in evidence as it has been taken up by a wide mouth to Martin's Lane with a traffic island in the middle.

Martin's Lane

Then... The Welsh Congregational Chapel was built on the corner of Bryn Bank in Martin's Lane in 1901. They had been meeting in Vienna Hall, Brighton Street previously. The church was Welsh speaking only and the keeper in 1902 was a Mr Edward Jones. It existed until 1969 when it was demolished along with the English Presbyterian Church next to it. The congregation joined the Welsh Baptists.

Martin's Lane was possibly named after Captain Martin who lived at no 23 at one time. The shops shown include Smiths hairdressers, Dicks cycle and motor cycles, the forerunner to Wallasey Motor Cycles, and Faircloughs sweets and tobacconist, which also advertises a library. At the time of this photograph private libraries were not uncommon for there was one on the first floor of Boots in Liscard Road in the 1950s.

Elm Cottage was an attractive cottage on Martin's Lane which nestled between Christ Church and Springfield Terrace.

Now... The Welsh Chapel and church beside it were demolished in 1969 and houses were built on the sites.

Although there has been some modernisation of the buildings, they do remain largely the same. The house at the corner of St Mary's Street is just recognisable. The empty Wallasey Motor Cycles shop replaced Dick's cycles but it moved premises recently.

The church and Springfield Terrace are still there but Elm Cottage has been demolished and a purpose-built block of flats now occupies the site.

100

Keenan's Cottage and Mill Lane : Dinmore Rd.

Then... Keenan's cottage was opposite the water tower in Mill Lane and was occupied by Henry Keenan, b.1817 in Ireland, who was the caretaker and therefore the key holder of the Tower. This was a very important position as the first fire appliances were kept at the front of the water tower, so he was called in an emergency. In 1881 he lived there with his wife Ellen, her brother William Doughty and her niece Mary Ellen Kay. In later years Mary Ellen married Peter Smith and may have been the 'Granny Smith' when the cottage was nicknamed Granny Smith's.

St. Alban's Church opened in 1853 with the Archbishop of Westminster, Cardinal Wiseman, preaching the sermon. Owing to some structural defects, in 1913 – 14 substantial alterations to the building were needed. When these were completed the church was re-opened in August 1914 by Cardinal Logue. One of the long-serving priests at St Alban's was Father Higgins whose silver jubilee was celebrated in great style in the 1950s.

← Keenan's Cottage.

Start of Dinmore Rd., opp. water Tower.

Now... Keenans cottage was approximately where Dinmore Road is now. This road leads to Central Park. Mill Lane is a busy residential area with its own group of shops including the ones shown. It is no longer the leafy lane but a main thoroughfare leading to the motorway.

The view is different but St Alban's church still survives in the modern times. The houses on the far right are recognisable in the old photograph too.

Highfield House and Mill Lane Hospital

Then... This large, elegant house was set in its own grounds next to the fever hospital in Mill Lane and had several owners during its life. The most notable of these was Samuel Reece, b1836 in Hatton, Cheshire, with his wife and family. He was the founder of Reece's Dairy and Restaurant chain. He died in 1909. The house became the town's maternity hospital and was later replaced by the new, purpose-built Highfield Maternity Hospital. This was in use until Arrowe Park opened in 1981 when it became the Minor Injuries unit.

The hospital was built in 1886 as a Hospital for Infectious Diseases. It was extended several times and developed into a centre for the treatment of tuberculosis, a maternity hospital and later a geriatric unit. The original building was used for many years as administrative offices. The Anne Glassey Workshop was built towards the rear of the site to offer work and occupational therapy to former hospital patients who were recovering from tuberculosis.

Now... Highfield Maternity Hospital has been demolished and the area it covered is where the new pharmacy and car parks are located.

In 1981 when Arrowe Park was opened most of the services transferred from Mill Lane although non-emergency services are still available here. Most of the old buildings have been demolished and new ones house medical and welfare facilities as well as doctors' surgeries.

The Model Farm and St. Alban's Road

Then... The Model Farm was, until 1870, one of the few sources of employment in Wallasey. It had approximately 40 acres and was a serious 'hobby' of Henry Littledale, b 1803, who lived in Liscard Hall. The farm was fragmented across a large area with the piggeries near the end of Marlowe Road, the sheep farm on Wallasey golf links with the shepherd's house at the junction of Green Lane and the path from Leasowe Road. The milk, butter and cheese produced was consumed throughout the town and farm hands came from as far as Ireland and North Wales in the summer.

St Alban's Road in the 1950s was a quiet thoroughfare between Mill Lane and Wallasey Road. It consisted of rows of terraced houses and schools. Marymount Convent School and St Alban's School playgrounds faced it and there was also an orphanage opposite the church. In 1901 the St Alban's club thrived and next door, at No. 22, lived Isaac Perkins, b 1857, a steam roller driver, with his wife Charlotte, 7 children, his father and brother (also a steam roller driver).

Now... All that remains of Littledale's Model Farm is the Bailiff's house, in Eldon Road, which has a plaque outside as a reminder of what was once there.

Dominick House, which contains all the welfare offices, dominates this end of St. Alban's Road. The terraced houses have been demolished in favour of offices, car parks and access to delivery points for the shops of the Cherry Tree Centre. St Alban's Club still flourishes next to the primary school, having once been the school room.

St. Alban's Terrace

Then... This is the row of terraced houses known as St. Alban's Terrace, off Wallasey Road. In 1949 the first three houses were occupied by Philip McConkey, a shipwright, Alfred Jones and Thomas Moss. These were demolished when the Cherry Tree Centre was built.

The photograph shows the part of Liscard between St Alban's Terrace and St Alban's Road. The shop on the corner of St Alban's Terrace was S. Pritchard & Sons, described as removers, storers and packers, and had a slightly different use in 1949. Then it was Samuel Pritchard & Sons, funeral furnishers. The public house near the corner of St Alban's Road is the Castle Hotel which, in 1949 was run by Mrs Edith McQuone.

Central Market in Liscard was built on the site of Clairville Cottage which was occupied in 1920 by W.R.Caddock. In 1919 the town planners decided that a market was needed and this site was eventually chosen. There were about 20 stalls in a covered market area with many selling fresh produce. There was also a garage and a photographic studio.

Now... This was another street of terraced houses sacrificed to build the shopping centre. Wilkinson's has been built across the site, the rear of which leads to a communal area of stalls and coffee shop. There have been many changes over the years. Harold Williams, gents' outfitters, which had previously relocated from Liscard Road occupied one of these units. This is now empty.

Great changes have been made to this view. Wetherspoons 'Clairville' was built on the site of the Central Market and adopted the name of the cottage which stood there many years before. Either side of the pub are shops but, sadly, many are empty.

Boot Inn

Then... It is said that the Boot Inn existed as long ago as 1561. In 1861 Stephen Gibbons, b 1834 in Wales, was the innkeeper and was there for many years because he was still recorded as the landlord in the 1891 census. In 1861 he lived there with his wife Ann and daughter Mary. The building shown was demolished for road widening in 1925 after the new building was built behind it.

Opposite the Boot Inn was a group of shops including, in 1949, Bellis' sweet shop, Hugh Charlton, the grocer, and Boughey's, the estate agents. Further on, the ivy-covered houses had been replaced by shops with Leicester's, the stationers, taking a prime position The shop fronts extended into the front gardens.

Now... The outside of the Boot Inn looks almost the same as when it was built in 1925 but it has undergone changes over the years. Most recently the inside was refurbished and it was re-opened under the name Turnberry's. This was obviously not a popular move because it has now reverted to its original name "The Boot". But as it is now "To Let", how long will it be there?

Some changes have taken place here but the Boot Inn still stands and has returned to its old name. The timbered building next to it is behind the trees and was once the stables to the old inn. It has been the Rambi Day Nursery, known as Rambi House for many years. The properties that were houses still stand but have been altered to accommodate shops. A Stage school has replaced the off-licence, previously Leicester's, the stationers.

Belvidere Fields

Then... This view of St. Hilary's Church was taken when Belvidere Road was little more than a cart track and corn fields abounded in the area. The house on the skyline is in Claremount Road. In 1898 only two houses existed in Belvidere Road.

Now... This area in Belvidere Road has been turned over to playing fields. The house with the white gable is the one in the old photograph but now between it and the field are several roads including Shrewsbury Road, Uppingham Road and Radley Road.

Seaview Road

Then... As the town grew and the transport system increased there became a need for a further Tramways Depot, to supplement the Field Road sheds. This was built on the site of the old water pumping station in Seaview Road. Further alterations were made, to accommodate the transition from trams to buses and the sheds were extended. The main offices for the Transport Department were at the entrance to the depot, on Seaview Road.

Now... When the main reorganisation of the ~~severel~~ Boroughs took place in 1974 the depôt was no longer required because operations were transferred to Birkenhead. The site is now occupied by an ASDA store.

CHAPTER SEVEN

Wallasey Village

In 1811 Wallasey Village consisted of 94 families - 440 people lived in 68 houses. These houses were mainly made of local sandstone from the Breck quarry. Several of them were whitewashed and had thatched roofs. On the 1811 ecclesiastical census 65 of the 94 families were dependent on agriculture, 16 on trade, manufacturing and handicrafts and the rest were unspecified. Some incomes may have come from wrecking!

Cottage Hospital

Then... Wallasey Cottage Hospital opened in 1885 but was originally sited in St Georges Road in Byron Lodge, north of the school, from 1866 until that time. In 1952 it became the Wallasey Hospital for Women until it closed in 1980. It was then demolished and replaced by Nightingale Lodge.

Now... This building replaced the Cottage Hospital and is a group of sheltered apartments originally called Nightingale Lodge, presumably to remember the original use of the land. However, there were moves to change the name as it was not deemed appropriate for accommodation for older people and it became Claremount Court.

Old Ship Inn and Hillside Cottages

Then... When St Hilary's Church was destroyed by fire in 1857 the services were held in classrooms in Claremont School, but using 3 adjacent rooms was not satisfactory so the services were moved to the Wallasey Friendly Society Club Room at the Ship Inn. Between 1850 and 1860 the landlord of the Ship, named Richard Cooper, was arrested for stealing and killing sheep which grazed on the marsh. He was taken to the Sessions House in Liscard Road and found hanged the next morning.

These three old cottages, known as Hillside Cottages, were next to the Ship Inn and were occupied in 1911 by Robert and Catherine Webster, Jane Goodman and her daughters and Anne Barton. They had all lived there for many years.

Now... Although the Ship Inn still stands, in a somewhat altered form, the cottages are long gone and have been replaced by a car park.

The Breck Footpath

Then... This footpath, behind the elevated houses on Breck Road next to the Ship Inn, was one of the main access routes to the Breck and Wallasey Mill. The Breck was once very extensive but by 1814 it was enclosed due to the encroachment of houses on the open land. The stone from here was used to make Leasowe Road. The contractor cut the road through the rock from St. Hilary Brow to gain access as this was the nearest quarry.

Now... The small building behind the wall at the corner of the footpath has been demolished and the first part of the footpath widened for parking but the houses remain intact.

Millthwaite and Sebastopol Inn

Then... Millthwaite was erected by Mr G.H.Peers, founder of the Peer's Institute, a temperance social club for young men in St. George's Road. He was co-owner of the defunct Wallasey Mill which stood on this site on the Breck and built this home where the family lived until the 1960s.

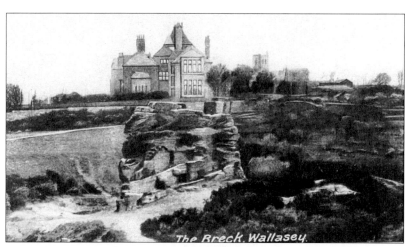

The photograph shows the Sebastopol Inn in 1920. It jutted out into St Hilary Brow. In 1859 the landlord was Richard Short. It was demolished in 1930 for road widening.

Now... The old house on the Breck, Millthwaite, was badly damaged by fire in 1968 and, as a result of this, was demolished. The site was used to build apartments named after the house and commanding the same view over the locality.

Now... The Inn was demolished and St Hilary Brow widened to accommodate the increase in traffic. The house which dominates this photograph can be seen at the side of the Inn in the old photograph.

The Old Cheshire Cheese

Then... The Old Cheshire Cheese was a low, thatched building with a later addition at the back facing up Church Hill so that it was L-shaped. From the photograph it can be seen that it had tiny windows and the steps to the door were worn and must have been a trial after a few beers. It was demolished in 1885.

The old Cheshire Cheese was behind where the horse is standing. Many cottages existed and the ones on the left were inhabited by various tradesmen including Stanley Strong, b 1870, a milk dealer, and his wife Maria.

Now... The present Cheshire Cheese was built in 1885 behind the old pub. A few of the licensees over the years were:- 1897 Eleanor Heeley Davy, 1912 Robert Edward Davies, 1946 Amanda Bryan, 1949 Matilda Taylor and, bringing it up to date, since 2003, Ken Robinson.

The flats on the left eventually replaced all the cottages which were demolished by the 1950s. Very obviously the road has been considerably widened in the modern day but the curve by the Cheshire Cheese is still evident.

Post and Panel Cottage

Then... This Post & Panel cottage diagonally opposite the Cheshire Cheese was the only surviving example of its type until it was demolished in 1921 to facilitate the widening of the road at School Lane. The owner, David Jones, was a newsagent and confectioner and moved his business into the premises which had been the Ring O' Bells Inn, at the corner of School Lane.

School Lane was once known as The Gutter and the name now used reflects the presence of the girls' school which was situated there. One of the old school teachers was Miss Railton, who came to Wallasey in 1859. Henry Carlisle, who was a warden at St Hilary's church, lived in an old thatched cottage here.

Now... The open road with houses behind shows where the old Post and Panel cottage once stood.

School Lane has been widened over the years and all the cottages have long since been replaced by the houses on the right and the flats on the left.

Broadway and St. George's Road

Then... Broadway was originally called Folly Lane or Folly Gutter. Beyond the hedges at the right of the photograph was a short cut to St Hilary's Church. The high wall was the perimeter of the large house Hilary Breck. The church shown is the replacement, in 1859, after fire consumed the original one in 1857 leaving only the tower. The Rev F. Haggitt, the minister at the time of the fire, was considered to be extremely brave because he took a great risk in saving the accounts and registers.

The first Grammar School was founded by the Parish of St Hilary probably in or near to the church and the first information on this is in 1595. A school was built on the north side of the church 1656-7 and remained until the building on Breck Road, now a private dwelling, was built in 1799. It is recorded that the schoolmaster in 1619 was paid the handsome sum of 20 shillings ie. £1 per year – paid in two instalments. In 1864 the school relocated to St George's Road, shown here, it was again re-sited to Withens Lane in 1876.

Now... This view shows the path by the library up to Broadway. The growth of the trees hides the fact that the large house Hilary Breck still stands at the side of the church. The small, winding path, which at one time led to the churchyard, no longer exists and has been swallowed up by one of the houses adjacent to it.

The school in St George's Road became an Elementary school for boys in 1876 when the Grammar school was moved to Withens Lane. In 1907 the school seen here was built on the original site and became the Primary school for the area. The school now boasts a nursery and has extended into the buildings vacated by Claremount School on Claremount Road. It is one of the largest primary schools in the country having around 800 pupils.

Parish Hall

Then... St Hilary's Parish Hall was a large building with side rooms, a stage and a balcony. It was used by church groups and was available for hire. The church Sunday School was held here and many families remember Auntie Jean with fondness. As it needed a large amount of money spending on it, the church decided to sell the land for redevelopment in the early 1990s.

Now... After the Parish Hall was closed the land was sold for building. These apartments, called Silverbirch Gardens now grace the site.

The Black Horse Pub and Websters

Then... The Black Horse was presumed to have been named after a famous horse which ran in the Wallasey Races. The old Black Horse was built in 1722 and was demolished after more than 200 years. The present building replaced it in 1931 and incorporated the original date plate.

These houses were numbered 83 and 85 Wallasey Village and, after being bomb damaged, were re-built for the Webster brothers who had an adjoining door between the two houses. In 1964 they were owned by the Hoylands and the Websters with F. Ledsham next door and Manley's, the chemists, to the right. The houses were sold and demolished for Kwik Save to be built.

Now... From the outside the Black Horse looks almost the same as when it opened in 1931. It has, however, been refurbished over the years and quite recently was renamed Sheridan's.

Kwik Save was on this site for many years until the company was sold to Somerfield, which is now part of the Co-op group. There is still a chemists on the right but McNay's has replaced Manleys.

Wallasey Village and Ward's Garage

Then... Ward's Garage was at the top of Leasowe Road between Irwins and the small police station. They also had a stores and showroom further down Leasowe Road. The garage was there during the period around 1937 – 58 but by 1964 it had been replaced by the Co-op.

On the right of this photograph, at the bottom of St John's Road stood the Hamilton Bros. bakery, which was built in about 1900. It was run by Thomas Hamilton, a Scotsman, b 1838, and later by his son James, b 1871. The Hamiltons were said to have built the first five houses in St John's Road and indeed descendants lived at No 3 until 2000.

Now... This shop has had many uses since the garage was demolished. It was a Co-op store for a few years in the 1970s and has also been a showroom for gas fires and surrounds. It has recently opened up as the pet shop seen here. The stores and showroom were replaced by shops, one of which was White's general store, which is now Cartridge World.

The view to the right of the photograph shows that the old buildings still stand. Hamilton's Bakery has changed use many times, from motor cycle shop, car showroom, estate agent and now a photography studio and framing point. The Bank building has lost its tower and is now offices. The shops on the other side of the road have been re-built further back than the original ones.

Leasowe Road

Then... Spragg's Brewery, known as Wallasey Vale Brewery, was on Leasowe Road. The proprietor was Richard Spragg b 1815 in Shropshire. He also leased the Black Horse at one stage from Mary Dean and passed it on to Jas. Westcott in 1859 stipulating that he buy the beer from Wallasey Vale. The beer, which sold for sixpence a pint in the bar, was not the only thing supplied by the brewery – so was the water for drinking and cooking. By 1881 Richard had died and his wife Emma had taken over as brewer with her son, also Richard, as her assistant.

Now... At one time Spragg's Brewery was the only building in this part of Leasowe Road. Now there are flats stretching from Mosslands Drive to the railway, and shops and the petrol station complete the buildings to the roundabout.

Wallasey Terrace and Twenty Row Inn

Then... The Twenty Row Public House was originally a small beer house at the end of a row of twenty cottages known as Wallasey Terrace. The landlord was William Ledsham who was also the village blacksmith. A new pub was built in front of the old house and then it too was demolished in about 2000.

Now... The Twenty Row public house was demolished when it became no longer viable as a business and fell into disrepair. After that there were applications for houses and a supermarket to be built on the site. Many objections to the supermarket were raised, including some from local Councillors and petitions from the Wallasey Village Community Group. Although it was refused at first the application was eventually granted and Lidl opened in September 2006.

Wallasey Village

Then... This is the group of properties between Leasowe Road and Beechwood Avenue which included the Wesleyan Chapel. This was in use between 1885 and 1910, when services were mostly conducted by local preachers. The building became a picturedrome for a short time in 1911-12 and was then replaced by shops.

Now... The building on the right still stands on the corner of Beechwood Avenue. In its time it has been many things from Bertie's supermarket to the present day video hire shop.

Wallasey Village

Then... Near to this terrace of houses was Puddle Cottage. This was so called because there was always a puddle in front of it and children enjoyed playing in it. Quayle's the chemists was the first shop after the cottages and was run for many years by Walter Quayle who was a relative of Anthony Quayle the actor. Notice the very early television aerials!

Now... The shop buildings still remain although their use is different. What was a chemist for many years is now a beauty salon called Complexions and to the right is Hardman's double glazing company. No cottages remain having been replaced by modern housing.

The Village Flood

Then... This photograph was taken during a flood around 1908. The shop shown is William Hemingway's barber's shop which was 149 Wallasey Village, a couple of doors up from the chemists Ernest Rogers. The first terrace house was occupied by Thomas Westcott, a joiner, whose remembrances of the Village were recently turned into a book.

This shows the shops and cottages from Beechwood Avenue along towards Sandy Lane. The corner shop had been a stationers since at least 1912 and the other end of that group of shops housed a chemists run by Ernest Rogers in 1912 and later by Walter Quayle.

Now... The photograph was taken from outside Complexions shop and shows that there is still a row of modern terraced houses which are set well back from the original line of houses.

The building on the corner of Beechwood Avenue is the only one recognisable in this photograph. The shop started out in the early days as stationers and has maintained that genre as it is currently a newsagents and tobacconists. Wendy and Kevin Harding owned it for many years until they retired.

Old Cottage near Big Yard

Then... There were several small cottages along the village with market gardens behind them. Although this cottage did not survive the rigours of time, the market gardens fared better and, in 1949, Herbert Jones ran his nursery from here.

Now... Big Yard was in use as a short cut from St George's Road to the village even when St. Mary's College was first built. However, it soon became obvious that members of the general public could not be allowed to walk through the school grounds and it was enclosed for school use only.

Wallasey Village

Then... This shows the group of cottages from Sandy Lane towards St John's Road including Laburnum Cottage owned by Thomas Sparks, b 1852, a market gardener who lived there in 1891 with his wife Hannah and children William and Thomas.

This painting shows an old scene in the village. The building prominent on the left, No 184, was owned in 1911 by Albert Tipping who was a decorator and contractor – perhaps illustrated by the white coated man busy at the side of the building. Just peeping out at the side is Laburnum Cottage.[1]

Now... St Mary's College was built on land previously occupied by the old cottages and market gardens.

[1] This picture is from a painting, the artist is unknown.

Hopps?

The Cosmo Cinema

Then... The Cosmo Cinema, known locally as the Cosy Cosmo, opened in May 1913 as a 700 seat cinema. Four shops made up the frontage of the building and there was an elaborate glass dome behind which a spiral staircase led up to the projection room. It was refurbished in 1924 and was re-named the Coliseum Theatre, which was bombed in 1941. On the side of the building to the left of the Cosmo is a sign advertising Spragg's Brewery, of Leasowe Road.

The Phoenix Cinema opened in 1951 on the site of the bombed Coliseum. It cost £40,000 to build and had a seating capacity of 930. It was one of the most popular cinemas in Wallasey but by the 1970s changes were made and 2 small cinemas and a bingo hall were created. This was not entirely successful and it closed in 1983 and was demolished in 1988.

Now... After the demise of the Phoenix Cinema in 1983 the building was boarded up and eventually demolished in 1988. A group of sheltered flats was built by Anchor Housing on the site.

Little's Shop

Then... Little's Shop, a newsagent and tobacconist, at 253 Wallasey Village was run in 1911 by Mrs Kathleen Faith Little, who came from Battersea, London. Her husband was Samuel from Toxteth, who, in 1912, owned a confectioners at number 241.

Now... The shop that was once Little's newspaper and tobacconists has now found a new life as a florist. The building has had some alterations carried out over the years.

Sandy Lane

Then... This view is looking up Sandy Lane towards Claremount Road. The church at the top is Claremount Methodist church, which was built in 1910, which replaced the Wesleyan Chapel in the Village.

Now... The narrow winding lane is only recognisable from the church at the top left of the photograph. Since the early print a tower has been added to the church.

Wallasey Village Looking North

Then... The picture shows, on the right, the buildings known as Mason's Cottages. These included two shops, the left hand one being run by Miss Mason who was celebrated for her black puddings.

Now... The wide road and part of the grounds to St Mary's College are all that can be seen now. The spire of the Presbyterian Church peeps above the shop building.

Granville Terrace

Then... Gotthold Johann Frederich Krueger, b 1846 in Germany, who was known as The Wallasey Hermit, lived in one of these houses. Later he lived the life of a recluse in a tin shack at the bottom of Green Lane. He was so well respected that when he died the people of Wallasey Village clubbed together to pay for his burial, in Rake Lane cemetery, to avoid his being buried in a pauper's grave.

Now... The terraced houses have been replaced by more modern housing. It is now known as Wood Lane.

Grove Hotel and Harrison Drive

Then... This picture shows the hotel and café in their heyday before being ravaged by fire. The café was owned by Samuel Reece and his sons, who lived in Highfield House. The Grove Hotel opened in about 1909 as a temperance hotel. In the 1950s the upstairs was transformed into the Melody Inn Club until it was badly damaged by fire in the 1960s. Shops incorporated into the ground floor premises included Longworth's cycle

shop, owned by George Longworth, b 1921, who lived in St George's Road. He continued to sell and maintain cycles until he was almost 80 years old.

Before Harrison Drive embankment was built the sand was blown from a line of dunes on to the railway line causing many problems. This was the reason for Warren Station being closed. The new road was opened in June 1901 to provide an extension from Wallasey Village to the shore.

Now... After the demolition of the fire-ravaged Grove Hotel this site remained derelict for a long time. It had a short life when a small factory unit operated from here and more recently has been developed into 'Village Living', which is a group of luxury apartments.

Harrison Drive has retained its open aspect. The main promenade was extended to include it by 1939 after the King's Parade was completed. There has been some residential property built on a small estate on the sea side of the railway line and the houses on Coastal Drive have been there for a number of years now. However, the promised development in the dips never materialised and the Wallasey Golf Club course, miniature golf and West Cheshire Sailing Club have kept the feeling of open spaces very much alive.

Derby Pool

Then... The Derby Pool was the successor to the sea bathing station and was opened by Lord Derby in 1932. It was situated at the Harrison Drive end of the promenade and was a favourite with the local people who often preferred it to the New Brighton Bathing Pool which attracted more day trippers. On a hot summer's day the floor of the balcony became so hot it was difficult to walk without burning your feet.

Now... After the Derby Pool was demolished all that remains today is the large grassed area. In 1977 planning permission was granted for a Fun Factory and licensed restaurant near the site. This has since been built approximately where the car park was and its architecture is a reminder of the once popular swimming pool.

CHAPTER EIGHT

Leasowe, Moreton and Saughall Massie

Leasowe

The name 'Leasowe' comes from the Anglo-Saxon Leasowes or 'Meadow (Lea) Pastures'. Its sand dunes are the largest such system on the Wirral. Much of the area is at or below sea level and is protected by the coastal embankment. Leasowe common is still used today for leisure activities.

Around 1761 the area was known as 'The Upper Mockbeggar', and Leasowe Lighthouse, built in 1763, is the oldest brick-built lighthouse in Britain. The lighthouse now has a visitor centre and is open to the public.

On Leasowe Road is the first building in the world to have been heated entirely by solar energy. The 'Solar Campus' was formerly St. George's Secondary School.

The world's first passenger hovercraft service commenced operations on 20th July, 1962, between Leasowe and Rhyl in North Wales. However, the service was not profitable and soon ceased.

The estates around Leasowe have been going through a time of refurbishment and modernisation. The old library has gone and has been replaced by the Millennium centre. In the 2001 census there were 6180 people living in Leasowe.

Brickworks and Gardenside

Then... Many brickworks have existed in Wallasey in the past. This one, Messrs Barker & Jones, in Leasowe Road, opened in 1892 and was purchased by R.P. Barker and Thomas Jones in 1900. In 1913, 130,000 bricks were produced weekly, mainly manually, by 62 men. As mechanisation was introduced, the work force lessened to 49 and the production increased to 150,000. The company was still in production in the 1960s.

As late as 1964 , there were only 9 houses in Gardenside – all on the right-hand side of the road. One of these was occupied by William Wallace, a Customs & Excise officer, and another by Constable Edwin Griffin. Both had lived there since at least 1937. The whole character of the road changed with the gradual encroachment of the Leasowe Estate, off Twickenham Drive, which was started in the 1950s.

Now... On the site now is a housing estate in Heyes Drive and also open space for leisure activities.

The corner of Gardenside is now occupied by Our Lady of Lourdes Catholic Church.

Leasowe Shops and Twickenham Drive

Then... When the estate was built in the 1950s, these maisonettes were built, with the shops at ground level. In 1964 there was a Co-op store, R. Wolfenden, the newsagent, W. Bryan, the chemist and McCulla's, the bakers, to name but a few. Between these shops and Birket Primary School was a large pond and on occasions local men fishing here would catch eels.

Now... The site of the pond has been in-filled and is now grassed over. It is located behind the present day new shops. The site of the old shops and maisonettes is now a car park.

Birket Avenue

Then... This picture of Birket Avenue is rarely seen. After carefully studying maps we believe that these homes stood at the top end of Birket Avenue near Reeds Lane, between Reeds Avenue West and Farmside. This part of the estate was being constructed around 1926, with nearby Birket Close being built about 1932. The land was part of Reeds Farm according to the tithe maps of 1837-51.

These shops were built when the new houses were being erected from around 1928 onwards. They consisted of a Co-op grocer's, Chemist, Post Office, Butcher's and Greengrocer's. Tommy Edwards, who ran the greengrocer's opposite the Co-op, was quite a character and served the community, along with his wife Grace and family, for many years from around 1942. After the deaths of his parents Jeff Edwards took over and he finally left in the 1970s. They also had a "VEG VAN" that they used to travel about in, serving the Leasowe estate.

Now... Although the shops are still there they have been upgraded and modernised. To the left in the picture are the newer houses that have been built along Reeds Lane, towards Ditton Lane. A large housing estate incorporating the shops at the end of Birket Avenue has been built on the land surrounding Reeds Farm.

Leasowe Station

Then... Although a single line track had been built between Birkenhead Docks and Hoylake, with a station at Moreton, this did not prosper at first. However, the connection with Liverpool in 1886 had a beneficial effect on its prosperity. Leasowe Station was built in 1894, when the single line was being converted to a double track with level crossing gates at Reeds Lane. The line was electrified in the 1930s.

Now... The Station House was eventually demolished and a new station office built. The old gates have been removed and a new, modern level crossing installed. A bus station and car park have been constructed to accommodate travellers.

Long Acre Cottage, Reeds Lane

Then... On the 1837-51 Tithe maps Thomas Smith is listed as the occupier of this cottage. By 1861 Rachel Smith was head of the house and lived here with her 5 children. The cottage stood on Reeds Lane, in front of Reeds Farm which was run by John and Mary Sutton in 1861. It was built in 1815 and demolished in 1934 just as the housing estate behind it was being built.

Now... A housing estate was built on this land to accommodate some of the people who lived in the caravans and wooden houses in the fields near Pasture Road and other fields close by.

Leasowe Hospital and Leasowe Castle

Then... Leasowe Road was little more than a lane, known as Leasowe Castle Road. In the distance can be seen what was, in 1911, The Liverpool Open Air Hospital for children, 'Leasowe House'. In 1911, there were also several houses and cottages with interesting names: 'Glan Mor' was occupied by Fanny Beilby and 'Veolan' by Robert Towers, a fishmonger. The Buffet Cafe on the corner was run in 1901 by Miss Emma P Sargent (sic. born c1864) who originally came from Northamptonshire. On the 1911 census, Mrs Jane Quillam (nee Sargeant),was listed as the manageress.

Leasowe Castle is said to have been built as early as 1593 and was possibly just one octagonal tower which was a good vantage point for the Wallasey Races. Four square towers were added later and the stables erected between 1600 and 1642. This had become disused by 1700, and it became known as "Mockbeggar Hall", a term often used for an ornate but derelict building. The term "Mockbeggar Wharf" is still used for the adjoining foreshore. In 1802 it was sold to Mrs Boode, whose daughter married Edward Cust,(b 1794 in London,) In 1821 ownership passed to the Cust family, who refurbished and

extended the building, using panelling from the demolished Star Chamber at the Palace of Westminster, as well as oak from the submerged forest along the coast. After 1826 the building was used as a hotel for some years. Between 1911 and 1970, it became a railway workers convalescent home, and between 1974 and 1980 it was owned by Wirral Borough Council.

Leasowe Children's hospital was built for the treatment of non-pulmonary tuberculosis and the first part was opened 21 July 1914. Its official name was The Leasowe Sanatorium for Crippled Children and Hospital for Tuberculosis. The land was previously owned by the Webster family and farmed by the Beed family. Margaret Beavan (1877-1931) was the leading force behind getting the hospital built. Over the years it changed to include treatments for burns, skin grafts and arthritis. The hospital closed in 1979 and in 1981 it became a Christian Centre and later a Retirement home and centre for the handicapped .

Leasowe Hospital and Leasowe Castle

Now... New flats were built on the site after the land had been cleared and the old garage demolished. Traffic lights have been installed at this junction which has improved the road safety at this 'black spot'.

Once again Leasowe Castle has become a hotel and is now a popular venue for weddings and other family functions.

The hospital was demolished and new flats were built on the site. The old stone gate posts were saved and incorporated into the new wall at the front of the flats.

Leasowe Farm, Leasowe Road

Then... The farm was run by James and Margaret Handley in 1841 and by 1881 it was occupied by William and Jane Sutton.

Now... Leasoweside is named after this farm and a housing estate was built on the land in the 1950s. A small number of market gardeners, along the opposite side of Leasowe Road, still grow and supply local produce for the area.

Leasowe Lighthouse

Then... The Lighthouse, built in 1793, is the oldest brick-built lighthouse in Britain. It was one of four along the North Wirral coastline and was operational until July 1908. Mrs Williams, the only female lighthouse keeper in England at the time, is shown here with her daughters. She was in charge for the last 14 years of its working existence after moving from the Great Orme Lighthouse. When it ceased to function, she ran it as a tea house. It was offered for sale in 1929 but no-one was interested. Wallasey Corporation bought it for £900 in 1930. Mrs Williams continued to live there until her death in 1935.

Now... The Lighthouse is now open to visitors and an active 'Friends of Leasowe Lighthouse' has been formed by volunteers. Around the perimeter of the Lighthouse are remnants of the petrified forest, believed to be over 5000 years old, that have been removed from the foreshore.

Moreton

Moreton is located on the headland of the Wirral Peninsula, about 1 mile from the the embankment facing Liverpool Bay, between New Brighton and West Kirby.

Moreton (formerly Moreton cum Lingham) was a township within the Bidston Parish and became a civil parish in its own right in 1866. In 1928 the whole of Moreton was added to Wallasey. A number of roads were renamed at this time owing to the duplication with street names in Wallasey.

Morton(sic) is detailed in the Kingston Survey of 1665 (otherwise known as the Vyner Survey). The earliest record of the population is for 1545 when there were 21 families living there. These figures remained virtually unchanged for about one hundred years.

Moreton was a rural village of farms and cottages and in 1811 the population was 230, much larger than Birkenhead, and predominantly agricultural. A more significant increase in population happened after the First World War, rising to over 4000 people. Owing to the shortage of housing, this resulted in the growth of over 2000 shacks and caravans in the fields just off Station Rd, now Pasture Road, between Moreton Railway Station and the Lighthouse. These fields, like Fellowship Field, were subject to flooding many times. Around 1928 the clearance and demolition of the 'shanty town' began and the building of new homes, roads and laying new sewers started in earnest and carried on for many years.

The Old Palais de Danse

Then... The old Palais de Danse was situated in Pasture Road. It has had many different uses over the years and in the 1960s was a roller skating rink.

This picture shows the bridge over the River Birket in Pasture Road. In the middle of the group of shops is Pasture Creamery. In 1937, before they were numbered, the properties had names such as 'Lyndale' where Edwin Hughes lived and 'Fair Dale' where George Wharton, the station master, lived.

Now... The rink became The Apollo Club until it reverted to its dance roots. The house next door has been demolished and is now the car park for the Apollo.

The bridge has been upgraded over the years and the houses are still there. This view has not changed much except that the few shops by the bridge have disappeared, and the road has been widened.

Pasture Road

Then... Pasture Road was once called Station Road, for obvious reasons, and was the main route through the village. This photograph shows the small shops that had grown up over the years to gain trade from the people walking to the shore.

Now... Many buildings and farms have been demolished in Pasture Road, nearer to the Moreton Cross end, and replaced by various types of other businesses. Once you go over the bridge at Moreton railway station towards the lighthouse there are a few new buildings and some of the older houses can still be seen.

Moreton Station and Pasture Road

Then... The original Moreton Station was on a single track railway line. It opened in 1866 and, although it was not used much at first, by the time the connection through to Liverpool was made in 1886 it had grown in importance. The huts seen in the background were part of the 'Bungalow Town'.

Now... Moreton Railway Station is still operational and the factory, still known as "Cadbury's" by local people, has been built on the land beyond. A wonderful smell of chocolate would drift as far as Leasowe and over Moreton Cross depending on the wind direction! The factory has changed ownership a number of times and recently has been Premier Foods but is now Burton's.

Mary Ann's Lane and Ivy Farm

Then... Mary Ann Dodd, wife of John, an agricultural labourer, is seen in this photograph outside her cottage in Mary Ann's Lane.

Ivy Farm was situated on Station Road opposite Dial House and the British Legion. Between 1901-11 Thomas Bennett Parkinson and Ellen Parkinson (née Lamb) worked the farm. The original Ivy Farm was built in the 16th century. This old farm was pulled down when the road was widened in 1935 and a new farm built a little further along the road.

Now... The site of Mary Ann's cottage is now the garden of the Moreton Christian Assembly Church. Flats have been built on the opposite corner and the lane has been renamed Old Maryland Lane.

On the site of Ivy Farm now is Moreton Library, which stands opposite a group of shops, the British Legion and Bells Funeral Directors (Dial House).

Garden Lane and Station Road

Then... Garden Lane contained a row of 7 terraced houses which was known as Moreton Terrace and there was a family butcher's and greengrocer's shop on the Station Road corner.

Job Thomas, born around 1840 in Farndon Cheshire, was described as a baker and grocer in the 1901 census. In 1911 Job's four sons helped him to run the businesses on Hoylake Road and Station Road.

Now... On this site now is a small car park for local shoppers.

Today the shop on Pasture Road is a betting shop.

Barnston Lane

Then... Barnston Lane was previously known as Chapel Lane. The houses on the right are Braywood Villas where, in 1937, Alfred Tarrant, a painter, and Thomas Astbury, a fitter, lived. The property next door to these houses is Yew Tree Farm, owned by Albert Parkinson in 1937. It was demolished in the 1950s.

Now... The first three old houses to the right of the picture remain today. Directly opposite is the property known as Old Hall Farm, which is the oldest house in Moreton, dating back to 1719, having been built for Daniel and Mary Wilson. It is now used as a care home.

Birkenhead Road and Station Road

Then... The original Coach & Horses public house was built in the early 1800s and was one of the many pubs owned by The West Cheshire Brewery. Their dray is seen in the photograph. This brewery, along with Birkenhead Breweries, was one of the oldest in this part of the country. The pub was demolished in 1928 to be replaced by a new, larger building in order to widen the road.

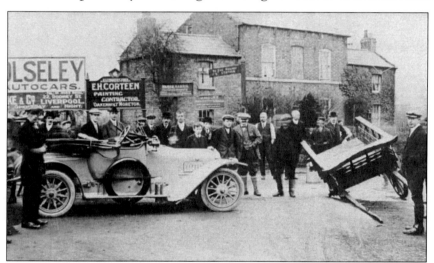

This group of men are obviously appreciating the sight of an early motor car. In 1911 Edward Corteen, born 1884 in the Isle of Man, was a painting contractor, according to his advertisement. He and his brother John boarded with the Birch family in "Oakenholt", Main Road, Moreton. Another of the signs in the picture says that Mary A Harris was a certified midwife.

Now... At Moreton Cross, opposite the Coach and Horses public house, stands the HSBC Bank and various other business premises.

The Smithy

Then... William Jebson Rimmer was the owner of this smithy on Birkenhead Road in 1911, employing his two sons and also Thomas Mutch, who lived at 4 Morgans Lane, which was later renamed Netherton Road.

Birkenhead Road, also known as Main Road, was a rough track leading from Moreton to Birkenhead. This view includes the site on the left where the Sacred Heart Roman Catholic Church was built in 1957, at the corner of Sandbrook Lane. The shop on the right was a grocer's and also housed the first Post Office in Moreton. It was run by Mrs Ellen Usher and was at the corner of Park Road and Birkenhead Road.

Now... This is the site of the old smithy and Mrs Usher's shop. Birkenhead Road is now Hoylake Road and Park Road is now Knutsford Road.. On the left of the picture the corner of Sandbrook Lane and a small portion of Sacred Heart Roman Catholic Church can be seen.

Chapelhill Road and Hoylake Road

Then... This white thatched cottage was one of the few properties in Hoylake Road but, sadly, it fell into disrepair and was demolished. In 1901 the "White Cottage" was the residence of Joseph and Margaret Richards.

Now... The house and shop on the left is at the junction of Chapelhill Road and Hoylake Road. It has had several owners but is still a newsagent's and general store.

Rudkin's Shop, Moreton Cross

Then... William and Helen Rudkin lived here, at 'Carbeen', and William is listed as a 'Fruiterer' in the 1911 Kelly's Directory. Mr Rudkin is the tall man in front of his wife Helen. Their son, Tom, is to the right on his bicycle. This row of shops, next to Sacred Heart Catholic Church, has name plates, between the top windows, commemorating horses belonging to Tich Mason, one being 'Carbeen' above Rudkin's shop. These horses were winners of local races.

Now... The name plates can still be seen today.

Hoylake Road

Then... This cottage stood at the corner of Hoylake Road and Holt Avenue. After it was demolished the Birkenhead & District Co-op was built on the site.

Now... Today it is a 'Home Bargains' general store.

Moreton Church of England School

Then... Moreton Church of England School was situated on Hoylake Road. The building of the original two-roomed school commenced in August 1860, the land being given by J R Shaw Esquire of Arrowe Hall. It was opened on 21 February 1861 when four scholars were admitted, rising to sixty three by March. A third room was added in 1866. The bricks used were hand-made from a marl pit on Birkenhead Road. The school was demolished in 1975 after the pupils had been relocated to the Upton Road buildings that were formerly known as Moreton Secondary Modern School.

Now... A general store and supermarket now stand on the site of the school. There is a short length of the old wall still standing on the left hand side.

Saughall Massie

Looking at Saughall Massie today you would wonder what has changed over the years apart from the shrubs and trees being more established, because the village has remained a quiet rural area.

Saughall Massie was once a township within the Bidston Parish, and became a civil parish in 1866. In 1933 the Three Lanes End area was devolved to Grange in West Kirby and the remainder was incorporated within the borough of Wallasey. The population was 98 in 1801, 176 in 1851 and 186 in 1901. Some of the surnames associated with the village are Wilkinson, Bennett, Broster, Brassey, Smith, Godwin, Harrison and Morgan to name a few.

The village consists of a number of historic buildings dating from the seventeenth century. In order to help preserve its historical and agricultural characteristics, Saughall Massie was designated a conservation area in January 1974.

Saughall Massie Village

Ivy Cottage is on the right of this picture and the white building on the left is the Saughall Hotel. They are both situated at the main road junction of the village and epitomise the air of peace and tranquillity of the area.

Diamond Farm, Poplar Farm and Saughall Hotel

In 1911 John Wilkinson (born about 1862 in Saughall Massie) and his wife Elizabeth and their five children worked the farm. The date plaque outside has the initial H / T & E 1728 for Thomas and Elizabeth Harrison who were earlier occupiers and raised a very large family at the farm. Diamond farm is still in the village.

A date plaque can be seen on the house which has P / D & M 1731 recorded. A Daniel Peacock was baptised in St Oswald's Parish Church Bidston on 29 November 1694 and a Daniel Peacock, aged 85, of Saughall Massie, was buried at the same church in January 1777. It seems likely that the Peacock family lived in this house. In 1911 Joseph Wilkinson (born about 1871 in Saughall Massie) and Hannah were the farmers who worked this farm. Most of the land has been sold now and a small housing estate has been built on land to the rear of the farmhouse.

In 1911 Jane Bird Whittaker, who was formerly married to William Mealor, was the licensee of The Hotel, later known as The Saughall Hotel, situated opposite Poplar Farm. Alterations have been made over the years. In the 1950s – 60s the licensee was Mr Henderson. It is now known as "The Saughall" and the present licensees are Mr Alan and Mrs Bernie Miller who have been there since about 1995.

The Elms

The Elms is situated between Diamond and Poplar Farms. The date plate on the house says S / G & A 1670. These initials could relate to one of three families who were in the area at about that time, George and Ann Sutton, George and Ann Smith or a family by the name of Sefton.

Although the house on the left shows some slight modification the chimney pots remain intact.

Ivy Cottage

Ivy Cottage has changed very little but has been improved and well maintained. There is a date plate on one of the gable ends that shows G / A & E 1690 for Arthur and Ellen Godwin (Godwyn), a yeoman. Joseph and Sarah Broster were living in the cottage in the 1940s. Joseph was a market gardener and worked the land for many years.

Thomas Brassey Bridge

Then... Saughall Massie Bridge was the first bridge constructed by the notable Victorian civil engineer Sir Thomas Brassey in 1829.

Now... The Thomas Brassey bridge was awarded Grade II listed status by English Heritage in 2007. A plaque commemorating this event was unveiled and an information board erected nearby.

Subscribers' Names

Mr Geoff and Mrs Angela Adams
Mr Peter Aherne
Mr Robert J Anderson
Mrs Sylvia Arden-Brown
Mr Steven and Mrs Ann Aspinall
Mr R J Astle
Mr Geoff A Baker
Ms Jane Beattie
Mr David L Beck
Mr Peter Behan
Mr Andrew and Mrs Stacey Bennett
Mr Ian J and Mrs Wendy S Bennett
Miss Jennifer E Bennett & Mr Phillip Warrington
Mr Joseph Bennett
Mr Colin and Mrs Sheila Beynon
Mr Colin R and Mrs Teresa C Birch
Mr David G and Mrs E Irene Birch
Mr D J Bratley
Mr David J Callaghan
Mr John Carroll
Mrs Heather M Chapman
Mr R Clough
Mr Michael E and Mrs W Colebourne
Mrs Gwen Collinson-Stokes
Mrs Margaret Dann
Dr Benedict Davies
Mrs Bunny Davies
Mrs C J Anne Davies
Mr Christopher Davies
Mr and Mrs N J Davies
Mr Paul Davies
Mr Richard Davies
Mrs Margaret Doughty
Mr David Dyer
Mr Terence Edgar
Mrs Joan Edwards
Mrs Joan Ellis
Mr David and Mrs Rona Ellison
Mrs Susan Euers

Mrs Sheila Fidler
Mrs Linda Finnigan
Mrs I Fletcher-Brewer
Mr Walter Forsyth
Mr Keith A and Mrs Margaret Foulkes
Mrs Beverley Gates-Price
Mrs Pamela J Gibson
Mr Roger H and Mrs Helen M Gill
Mrs Angela Goodman
Mrs Marie Gretton
Mr Andrew Hamilton
Mrs H Sheila Hamilton
Mrs Margaret Ann Harding (nee Hignett)
Mrs I Healing
Mr Karl Held
Mr Alan and Mrs Audrey Henderson
Mr John Henshaw
Mrs Maureen Higgins
Mr Jack and Mrs Marion Hill (USA)
Ms P A Hill
Mrs Joy Hockey
Mrs Joan Hodgkin (Canada)
Mrs Beryl Holden
Mrs Gladys Houghton
Mr Leslie H Howard
Mr Dylan and Mrs Suzanne Howell
Mr John Irvine
Mrs Eliza Ivison
Mrs Iris Johnson
Mrs Olwen R Jones
Mrs Beryl Jordan
Mr Peter V Jordan
Mrs Joan Kendrick
Mr Sidney M King
Mrs Ann Lakin
Mrs Agnes E Lea
Miss Dianne B Lea
Mr Stephen A Lea
Mrs Janette Lyon
Ms Sasha McCann
Mr John and Mrs Jo McCourt
Mr Robin Alexander Nettleton
Mr George H Nichols
Mr Alan and Mrs Sheila Nicholson
Mr Harry Nickson
Mr Ronald Norris
Rev. L A J Ostaszewski

Mr John Pearson
Mr Brian Perry
Dr Ian and Mrs Vicki Pickering
Mr Peter Platt
Mrs Phyllis Ponton
Mrs Patricia A Pritchard
Mr David G and Mrs Sheila Pugh
Mr Andrew Rae
Mr David Railton
Rev. Mary Railton-Crowder
Mrs Kay Redmond
Mrs Barbara Reid
Mrs C M Richardson
Mr Robert S Riley
Mrs M Joan Rivett
Mrs Alison J Robb and Mr Peter Etherington
Mr and Mrs C Robinson
Mr John and Mrs Diane Robinson
Mr Jeffrey T Robinson
Mr Ian C and Mrs Barbara A Samples
Mrs Norma Scregg
Mr Kenneth D and Mrs Brenda Sharpe
Mrs Anne Shaw
Mr Noel E Smith
Rev. Joe Speakman
Mrs Cynthia P F Speed
Mrs Gail P Thomas
Mr John Timms
Mr Roger H Trapnell
Mr James F Varty
Mr George Walker
Mr Graham Walker
Mr I Walker
Mr Tom and Mrs Janet E White
Mrs Margaret Evers Wiese (USA)
Mr Alan L Wilkinson
Mr Phil G Worthington
Mr Douglas Wright

Index